1-20-69

WHERE RELIGION GETS LOST
IN THE CHURCH

WHERE RELIGION GETS LOST IN THE CHURCH

by

C. EDWARD CROWTHER

MOREHOUSE-BARLOW CO.

NEW YORK

For PAUL, ALISON and DEBORAH,

for whom the Church of today

may become their world of tomorrow.

ACKNOWLEDGMENTS

Grateful acknowledgment is given to the following publishers and authors for permission given to quote copyrighted material from the titles listed.

A Time for Christian Candor, by James A. Pike. Published U.S.A. 1964, Harper & Row, Publishers, Inc.

New Delhi Report, The Third Assembly of the World Council of Churches. Published England 1962, S.C.M. Press.

Christian Responsibility in One World, by A. Theodore Eastman. Published U.S.A. 1965, The Seabury Press, Inc.

The Archbishop's Test, by E. M. Green. Re-issued U.S.A. 1960, Morehouse-Barlow Co., Inc.

The Lambeth Conference Report. Published England and U.S.A. 1958, S.P.C.K. and The Seabury Press, Inc.

God on Monday, by Simon Phipps. Published England 1966, Hodder & Stoughton Ltd.

The Church Reclaims the City, by Paul Moore. Published U.S.A. 1964, The Seabury Press, Inc.

Lay People in the Church, by Yves Congar. Published U.S.A. and England 1964, Newman Press and Geoffrey Chapman Limited.

8 ACKNOWLEDGMENTS

New Patterns for Christian Action, by Samuel J. Wylie. Published U.S.A. 1959, The Seabury Press, Inc.

A quote made by the Rev. Canon Philip H. Cecil from *Church Quarterly Review,* July-September, 1966.

With Love to the Church, by Monica Furlong. Published England 1965, Hodder & Stoughton Ltd., and U.S.A. 1968, Forward Movement Miniature Books.

Sex and Morality, a report to the British Council of Churches. Published England and U.S.A. 1966, S.C.M. Press, Ltd., and The Fortress Press.

The Comfortable Pew, by Pierre Berton. Published Canada and U.S.A. 1965, McClelland and Stewart Ltd., and J. B. Lippincott Co.

CONTENTS

PROLOGUE

On June 30, 1967, I was arrested by officers of the Special Branch of the South African Police, held in custody for several hours, placed on a London-bound plane, and deported from the Republic of South Africa.

No charges were made, no allegations which could be adjudicated by a court of law were presented. The only reason offered on my mimeographed order of deportation was that my presence in South Africa was no longer "in the public interest." It is a reasonable assumption that the basic reason for my removal was the criticism of apartheid which I had consistently made, within and outside South Africa.

What the Church has constantly proclaimed I passionately believe: racism is a blasphemy against the fatherhood of God and the brotherhood of man. My experience, first as a parish priest and then as a bishop in South Africa, convinces me that here is a repressive system of government which causes untold hardship and misery to the fifteen million non-white citizens of that republic. On theological and humanitarian grounds, the political creed of white supremacy is wrong in theory and vicious in practice.

It may be that silence or even compromise is the most "diplomatic" form of opposition. At least, it is said, such a course presents the opportunity to work for justice quietly within the system, and to remain in the country ministering to the spiritual needs of one's people. For some, such a course no doubt is possible. For me, it was neither possible nor right. I believe that the prophetic ministry of the Church requires that the world's attention be drawn to injustice and oppression wherever it is found. If the wrath of government is incurred as a result,

11

such a consequence has ample precedent in the Church's history.

The wrath of Pretoria, however, is not directed exclusively against those who are "too outspoken." Now the Anglican bishop who perhaps more than any other has tried to avoid political confrontation with the South African authorities has been ordered to leave. Robert Mize, for nine years Bishop of Damaraland, a vast diocese covering South West Africa, has ministered pastorally to his predominantly black African people. The presence of this gentle man is no longer tolerated by the South African government. In violation of the original mandate, and in defiance of the United Nations' resolution of 1966 that denied Pretoria any jurisdiction in South West Africa, Bishop Mize has been ordered to leave the country. Perhaps the common denominator for the expulsion of both Bishop Mize and myself is the fact that we are both American citizens. Certainly the advocates of the politically uninvolved ministry in South Africa will now have to reassess the efficacy of their method of survival. Perhaps some of them may even wonder why they are allowed to remain!

The Church is big enough to encompass both the pastoral and the prophetic ministries. I hope and pray that neither ministry gains a monopoly of concern so as to eliminate the other.

This book, however, is not an account of my experiences of apartheid in South Africa. That story will come in a later publication now being written. The manuscript of this present book was completed before my deportation. Quite deliberately, it has not been updated or materially changed. The concerns which are expressed are to me as valid now as when they were written. Many of the problems resulting from inflexibility of Church structures and doctrines, seem even all the more and disturbing now that I am no longer in the "missionary" situation out of which the book speaks.

The Church in the United States, in Britain, and everywhere else I have visited since my deportation, is faced with problems similar to those raised in this book. Wherever it is uttered, "black power" is the cry of disillusionment from the depth of long-frustrated hope that the white man will ever really voluntarily change. It is a cry that will be heard increasingly throughout the world.

The search for an expression of spirituality is one of the generating motives of the "hippie" movement. The institutional Church is a part of the society which is rejected by those who seek to contract out of the "establishment" and all that it connotes.

Meanwhile, the war in Vietnam escalates and divides nations into hawks and doves. The division splits the Christian community, too, and so the clear cry for peace and good will among men which should come out of the Church is muted. At a time in history when the greatest possible mobility and flexibility are called for, the Church seems to be immobile and inflexible. Reforms there have been, but they do not approach the massive revolution needed within the Church if she is to act, instead of react, to the contemporary condition of the world. The underground church is taking form. Whether it will be far enough removed from those ecclesiastical structures that apply the brakes, rather than accelerate change, may well determine the institutional Church's ability to survive.

This book was written in the front line of man's bigotry and intolerance of his brother's aspirations to equality and justice. It is an attempt to share my own frustrations and hopes. What comes out of South Africa may stimulate dialogue outside. My deportation may present a real-life situation which has considerable teaching opportunities if the Church can use it. There is a price to pay for witness, and sometimes the price is high, but as Christians we are not entitled to suffering at a discount.

In one sense, my removal from South Africa is a hopeful sign. When a government can no longer tolerate any man's interpretation of what the Christian gospel means in action, at least the Church is seen to be alive!

C. EDWARD CROWTHER

The Center for the Study of Democratic Institutions
Santa Barbara, California

August 1, 1968.

PREFACE

The life of a bishop is a busy one—often too busy. This book is an attempt to reflect my own concerns about our busyness, and, if I preach a cause, I preach it to myself. To write a book is a worthwhile experience, if only to the author. One is compelled to study and to reflect, to develop and to refine attitudes and opinions. To the diocese of Kimberley and Kuruman I have tried to bring much that was given to me by the American Church. Now, from my experience in South Africa, I seek to offer something in return.

My gratitude is due to many kind friends who have encouraged me to write.

To Dr. Betty Eisner, of Los Angeles, who taught me that often "seeing is believing," and that this applies to oneself before others can be loved.

To Miss Jill Molineaux who, as my secretary when I was chaplain at U.C.L.A., and more recently in Kimberley, has shown to me something of the virtues of loyalty and patience. If the Church paid overtime for hours worked, Jill could retire tomorrow!

To my friend and chaplain, Peter Beech, who has made many suggestions for improvement of both my life and manuscript. Remaining defects in each are not his fault.

Finally, to my wife Margaret, my words of thanks fade into insignificance beside her sharing of all that has produced this book. To share my life anywhere is no easy task. Especially is this true in South Africa. When I say that she appears to enjoy it, that is praise indeed!

C. EDWARD CROWTHER

Bishopsgarth
Kimberley, South Africa

WHERE RELIGION GETS LOST
IN THE CHURCH

I

TODAY'S WORLD—
CHALLENGE OR THREAT?

 JUST WHAT has the Church to offer
to a contemporary society dramatically engaged in probing
both the reachable limits of outer space and of the inner mind?
Whatever form our offering might take, it is made to a society
spiritually and politically fragmented to be sure, but with a
technology capable at the same time of massive destruction
and almost miraculous healing.

It is not only the spiritual and technological condition of
man which we must consider. Where man physically is to be
found is vital too, if we are to be incarnational in our approach.
Man is constantly pushing outward in exploration, knowledge,
and exploitation of both natural and human resources. Increasingly, he also becomes concentrated into concrete cities.

In America, we see the growth of the megalopolis, sweeping
upward to the sky and pushing its roots deeper into the
earth. We scrape the skies and burrow into ever bigger holes.
Throughout Europe, the cities are growing, absorbing and
swallowing up communities which a few years ago were rural
enough to be summoned to worship by the sound of their own
church bells. In Africa, too, urbanization has come to stay and
is creating the usual problems, with, of course, African addi-

tions. Everywhere, established social patterns evolved through the centuries are being swept away and replaced by the concept of instant community. It is easy to see the pressure for change as a threat, and the institutional church is particularly vulnerable to such a temptation.

The change for the black African is perhaps more brutal than for the Englishman or American. Effects of the industrial revolution, which have been evolving in England since the late eighteenth century, are only now becoming really obvious in Africa. Yet, at the same time as the African is being caught up in the tentacles of the city, the cry of apartheid in South Africa is "back to the homelands." The creation of bantustans, or strictly African areas for the African,[1] is diametrically opposed by the necessity of economic integration. The demand of the cities for cheap labor seems to be insatiable.

Of all the victims of urbanization in the world, the black South African must rank as a top candidate for creative sympathy. He is torn in two by the rival claims of political ideology and economic demand. The implementation of apartheid, that is, of the separate development and legislated segregation of the races, requires that he be pulled out of the city. The continued expansion of South Africa's rapidly growing industries demands that he be kept close by. But yet he is not really in the city, even when economics wins. He is available in outlying townships which themselves create problems of African urbanization, superimposing themselves on the problems of the all-

---

[1]In the African languages "Bantu" means "person." In South Africa the term "Bantu" is used to designate all black Africans whatever their tribal nation. Of the eighteen million citizens of South Africa, over thirteen million are black Africans who prefer to be known simply as "African." Approximately three and a half million are whites who are officially called "European." Slightly over two million are of mixed ancestry and are known legally as "colored," a very general designation which in popular use also includes Indians, Malays, and Asiatics—anybody in fact who is neither black nor white.

white cities. The "urban African," who for generations has not known his tribal home, is out of sight and sound so far as the real city is concerned. He lives with his own people to satisfy the demands of apartheid. He is available, however, always available, for the white man's industries to feed upon.

In his book, *The Church Reclaims the City,*[2] Paul Moore has pointed out the need in the United States for the Church to revolutionize her approach to the inner city. So, too, in Europe, Africa and elsewhere throughout the third world, one of the most urgent needs is to rethink the way the Church's nature is expressed in terms of the societies in which she works.

If Anglicanism, for instance, is to survive, urgent liberation is necessary from the superimposition upon totally alien cultures of the Church of England as it was one hundred years ago. To replace the Queen with a synod simply will not pass as an honest attempt to indigenize the Church's structure. The sooner we realize this inescapable fact, the more realistic and therefore recognizable our offering of Christ will become.

As the Paul Report and other studies of the English Church have shown, many English churchmen themselves are convinced that the existing structure of the Church of England does not allow the Church to express her real nature even in England. Yet, in many parts of the world, the Anglican Church shares with many other imported Christian denominations the influence and image of a classic Victorian museum, the pathetic institutional survival of the British raj.

The basic need in Africa, for instance, is not to have more black African Archdeacons and Bishops as prized showpieces of ecclesiastical emancipation. To Africanize a totally outmoded system it is not enough merely to color black the English way of doing things and to call it African. We must truly

---

[2]Moore, Paul, *The Church Reclaims the City,* The Seabury Press, Inc., New York, 1964.

indigenize at the ground level. Obviously, this will involve the Church's music, her liturgical forms of expressing worship, her architecture, language, administration, and her whole ethos. In South Africa all these elements of the Church's life, with rare exceptions, are chips off the old English block. Indigenous people everywhere have their contribution to make if the Church is to be truly the people of God who have found their Christ.

To act as if we believe that this is so would revolutionize the appearance of the Church's mission overseas. Some very familiar faces and customs would be removed from the scene. The Church would be compelled to fall back on local resources which, in many places, by now are probably atrophied. At least, such a policy would present a realistic if harsh picture of where in fact Christianity stands in those areas where the Church has worked for generations. Missionary reports to the subscribers back home are not deliberately dishonest. They picture the situation, however, through foreign eyes. Success or failure in mission is often judged by the degree to which the natives have been taught to do things "our" way.

We must radically change our system of doing things, of expressing the nature of the Church at every level, so that the people themselves want, for instance, to create and build their own churches employing the structures of their own community, expressing themselves in their own language, music, and ritual. To be Christians, indigenous people anywhere do not have to accept what foreigners think they should like.

Out of Africa there can and *must* come something that is Christian and African. We cannot afford to allow Western forms of Christianity to be imposed on African culture much longer.

Christ is in Africa. Christ was in Africa, as He was everywhere else before the Church arrived. He does not have to be taken anywhere. To realize this fact is to understand something close to the very heart of mission. If there is a specific function of the missionary from overseas, it must surely be to meet and show forth Christ where He is already. We cannot expect only to find Him wearing a business suit, singing hymns in English, living in a mock-Gothic church. The ability to sing the Lord's song passionately is the Africans' gift to the frozen people of God. We must not make the African sing the Lord's song in a land which we have made strange. No, when there is singing or building to be done, it must be done *by* or *with* the African, not *for* him.

As has been done in Gaberones—the capital now being built in one of Africa's newest independent states, Botswana (until very recently a part of the Diocese of Kimberley and Kuruman)—the African should express what the Church's building should say to him. Of course, that is in Botswana. In South Africa, the land of apartheid, there would be many practical problems in allowing the black African free expression of *anything*.

Looking out of the South African window upon the Church elsewhere, one gains the impression that we Christians must be a great disappointment to the rest of the world. Only three years or so ago, I was looking into South Africa from the United States. What I expected to find, I do not discover now that I am here. The Christian Church in South Africa is in the very front line of Christ's confrontation with the sin of racism. Surely the Christian community in Southern Africa should act and not merely deliver pious talk and lengthy synodical resolutions.

If positive witness to the doctrine of the fatherhood of God and the brotherhood of man is indeed possible in this world, then Christians in South Africa should be providing it. Yet names do come to mind of Christians who have done more than talk in South Africa—Albert Luthuli, Michael Scott, Trevor Huddleston, Ambrose Reeves, Joost de Blank, to mention just a few whose names avoke memories of faded hope in the minds of African people.

There are few voices, and even fewer deeds, representing Christian action in South Africa today which speak and witness to the whole world in the area of race relations. The impetus of witness has passed to the United States. There, some Christian voices have helped activate a great movement which is certainly changing the history of the United States. In South Africa, we tend to say too easily: "But your situation in America is different from ours." This partly is true, of course. No two situations are the same. One of the biggest differences, however, is that so many Christians have joined with non-Christians in speaking with the voice of prophecy in both the North and South of the United States. What is more important, positive action has followed words. Had Martin Luther King been unduly concerned about unfavorable publicity or possible suffering, there would have been no civil-rights movement as it is known in the United States. Yet, it seems to be a characteristic of many Christian denominations to fight shy of publicity.

Sometimes in South Africa I am appalled at the fear expressed by Church leaders of publicizing words or deeds which oppose the racist policy of apartheid. Our utilization of modern means of communication is pathetic. At the end of many Church meetings there is the inevitable and rather amusing few moments of reflection as to what can be released or denied to the press. We act as if the news media were the enemies of Christian action. In fact, our inaction is infinitely more likely to be ignored than to be opposed.

In South Africa, the vast majority of people are deprived by inhuman laws of their basic human rights. In such a situation, the Church must present to the world her practical alternatives to the blasphemy of apartheid. In South Africa today the cost to the Church's own soul because of silence and inaction is too high.

Suffering resulting from Christian concern and witness is redemptive to the Christian. Such suffering is not to be shunned by the individual Christian in order to avoid the consequences of saying or doing what is right. Sometimes it is the Church's obligation to allow individual Christians the right to decide whether or not they will suffer for truth's sake. It is our duty to enable individual Christians to grow to meet the challenge of suffering by their freedom to respond to it. Often the duty of the leaders of the Church is to act in full knowledge that what we do may cause suffering to ourselves and to others.

For instance, very shortly after becoming Bishop of Kimberley, a situation arose which illustrates the point. The government required the segregation of the living quarters of a house and conference center. The particular institution was one of the few places where Christians of all races could live together under the same roof for a few days at a time. I pleaded that some point of confrontation was vital if we were not to be completely overwhelmed by apartheid. The preservation of at least a semblance of Christian community seemed to be one of the few remaining points not already sacrificed by the Church. Here we could make a united stand against apartheid. The decision was made, however, to conform to the government's demands. Because the Church had co-operated regarding her position, the blow was light and there was scarcely any noise. Yet another nail in the Church's coffin was hammered in by the South African government. Among several reasons given for the extraordinary decision to conform to official pressure was that it would be Africans who, if found under the same roof as white men, would be the ones to suffer most.

There were black African Christians who would have been

prepared to suffer if the Church had given them a worth-while opportunity. Here lies the tragedy of the Church's retreat from confrontation in South Africa. We deprive those Christians who are prepared to suffer the chance to grow in such an exercise of their freedom as choosing the path of defiance.

One grows weary of hearing the standard rationalization for constant retreat. "We cannot risk all-out confrontation with the government. Look at what happens to those who do publicly oppose. They are in jail or get deported and what is the good of that?" Such words have a hollow sound. Without the witness of those who were willing to take risks, the civil rights movement in the United States would never have begun, let alone gathered momentum. What does it do to the Church when she constantly retreats from confrontation with evil? What does our silence say to those who are voiceless and powerless to resist oppression? Our increasing silence and inaction speak with a shameful and frightening eloquence. The consequences to the life of the Church are far more serious than anything Premier Vorster can accomplish by his deportations and bannings.

The past history of the Church shows that she can take in stride all that Caesar can do and emerge from persecution strengthened and refined.

There is little danger of persecution of the Church in South Africa, however. We take ourselves too seriously if we imagine for one moment that Mr. Vorster and his watchdogs ever give a thought to the possibility of united Christian opposition to his racist policies. He knows from past experience that the protesters who could become dangerous can be picked off one by one. It is not surprising that the government of South Africa behaves accordingly. Christians are arrested, banned or imprisoned, bishops and priests are deported or have their passports withdrawn if South African citizens, and the voice of protest becomes weaker and increasingly disregarded.

It is very difficult indeed now to find any areas in which the Church has not sacrificed her ability to make a decisive stand against apartheid. We are told that the Church will really rise up, unite, and fight if Vorster's government ever seeks to inhibit inter-racial worship. In all too many cases, Mr. Vorster does not have to ban it. There are many parishes in which white Anglicans succeed in retaining racial purity beyond any capacity of Mr. Vorster's wildest dreams of enforced apartheid.

With rare exceptions, the ministry of a non-white clergyman to white Christians is almost unthinkable in South Africa. Provided that the requirements of the Group Areas Act are complied with, and that the colored or black minister resides in the area designated for his racial group, no law is broken by a non-white clergyman ministering to a white congregation. In the Anglican Cathedral in Kimberley, colored and black priests occasionally preach or celebrate the Holy Communion, and we have tried to ensure that white clergy do not travel a hundred miles and more on a Sunday to hold services for a few white parishioners who live within a mile or so of a non-white priest. The issue is not so much the refusal of white Christians to receive the sacraments from the hands of a black minister as the improbability that the need to make a decision to do so has ever arisen. The responsibility for such a state of affairs lies at the Church's door. The capacity to absorb the pain of separation in the Church itself seems to be unlimited. A white priest ministering to black people is taken for granted as part of the missionary mythology of Western Christianity. The idea that a black minister has anything to offer to his white brother simply is not one for which either black or white Christians in South Africa have been conditioned by the Churches.

In most Christian denominations non-whites are either discouraged from attending "European" churches, or are not allowed to do so. Where they are permitted to worship with whites, they are frequently seated at the back of the church or on one side of the aisle. Such physical separation in church is not the fault of the law which is silent on the subject of church seating arrangements! Responsibility for this state of affairs belongs to the leadership of the Churches concerned. The bigotry of white Christians has been tolerated for so long that it now possesses the force of custom. Small wonder that whenever the Churches speak out against the evils of apartheid the charge of hypocrisy is hurled in our faces. If in South Africa we cannot show that Christians of different races can sit together to worship God, it is hardly likely that our piety will inspire political society to change its ways. The psychology of servitude embraces both oppressor and oppressed. It is tragic that this truth can be seen in the rationalizations of so many Church members who appear to accept the unacceptable, and constantly feel the need to defend their choice. Even in churches where inter-racial worship is a long-established custom, such as in our Cathedral in Kimberley, the implementation of the Group Areas Act is slowly but surely dividing our congregations into segregated communities.

In the face of such developments, some of them caused by irresistible government policy and some caused by the Church's constant compromise, I do not see that as a Christian community we are sharing effectively in the witness of our brethren against racism elsewhere in the world.

Part of the failure, at least of the Anglican Church, must be attributed to the predominant position occupied by non-South African bishops and priests. For the greater part, those who are in any position to speak are on the right side of the fence of privilege. The sensitive white man hurts because he sees the suffering surrounding him. He cannot *feel* the whole pain himself. I believe that Jesus Christ does feel it and therefore so must His Church before the love through which the pain is transformed can be released. Again, perhaps the system under which the Church operates dulls or anesthetizes the pain of individuals. The cumbersome and alien institution is far too removed at the top from the everyday life of the people of God to really know and understand the volume of pain which exists.

As a Bishop, I shepherd my sheep, most of whom live in the veld, from a beautiful home in an exclusive white suburb. That is why the system of which I am a part anesthetizes the pain I should feel. Of course my voice is muted and of course my deeds seem dull to the black African living on the jagged edge of despair. In his day-to-day battle for survival he sees me come and go. I do not stay and live with him, so I cannot truly know and share his pain.

What a massive contribution to the world an African Christian Church could have made, and no doubt still could make if only the Church were big enough to take hold of the opportunities, but what a break with traditional alignments this would mean. We speak often about the Old Testament idea of the holy remnant being applicable to our day and time. Certainly, numerically, the Christian Church in most parts of the world is being cut down to a size which the term remnant suggests. But the prophet Isaiah saw the remnant of Israel as being something more than a simple remainder. The concept of remnant is that of the steel tried in the fire, purified and strengthened by adversity. In South Africa a ready-made situation exists in which a holy remnant could very well be all that would survive if the Church were true to herself.

One of our more sickening characteristics in South Africa, as I am sure elsewhere, is the way in which we rationalize our need for continued popularity. In describing the Anglican Church as "the most hated Church in Africa," Mr. de Wet Nel, then Minister of the Interior, was paying Anglicanism a profound compliment. Of course, in response, many of us said the right things about Christ not being judged by the popularity polls, and so forth. But how we fight shy of the ultimate consequences of the hatred of the world. Perhaps the Church in South Africa needs a few martyrs. Maybe a few more bishops will have to join Ambrose Reeves, late of Johannesburg, in exile, following their deportation. If that is the case, so be it. It *will* be the case when the Church rejects her traditional alignments with the class of privilege. This applies to South Africa, the United States, Britain, and wherever else our institutional form depends for its survival upon the support of the rich.

For its own good, the Christian Church must not be allowed to get away with the idea that "remnant" is a label merely to be attached to depleted numbers. There is no such short cut to corporate holiness. No, the remnant will be the spiritually fit who have paid the cost of survival out of the wealth of Christ's accepted love.

II

THE CREED THAT CAME IN FROM THE COLD

T HE CHRISTIAN SHOULD express, by his involvement in the living issues of this world, God's continuing concern for His creation. The Church should be a vehicle of involvement and Christian action in the world. The foundations of Christian activism are not merely sentimental and emotional reactions to injustice, however. They take their roots in what we believe about God. If what we do is not based upon what we believe, then our actions will be capricious and self-centered. So grounded, the most eloquent leadership in the most worthy causes will be unreliable and downright dangerous. The world is entitled to examine Christianity's credentials. By them, the validity of our speech or our silence, our action or our inaction, will be evaluated.

At first sight, mention of the doctrine of God does not seem to provide the most obvious basis for an examination of the Church's priorities. Maybe the apparent remoteness of the doctrine is an indication of why ecclesiastical priorities need drastic examination and revision. One of the great foundation stones of Christian faith is the truth that this is God's world. This is a truth which in our self-preoccupation it is all too easy to forget. Nevertheless, the sovereignty of God is at the very heart of the Church's being. God's nature as Creator, Redeemer, and Sanctifier is the ultimate cause of the Church's existence. Our measure of God's concern for the world is the fact that He created it. The basis of the Church's mission in the world today is that God through Jesus Christ redeemed, and, through the working of the Holy Spirit, continues to sanctify it. The existence of the Church is the manifest expression of God's continuing concern for His creation. Especially is this true for mankind, that human part of creation which can consciously and reciprocally respond to the love which brought it into being. Because God so loved the world, Jesus Christ came among us, and it is because He continues so to love the world that Christ remains with us in the form of His Body the Church.

The progress of man in acquiring knowledge often obscures the fact that we and the world we live in are God's creations. This is what we mean when we proclaim that God is King. With our emphases on the material and the physical it is not surprising that we should consider ourselves self-contained captains of our souls. Contact with realities such as birth and death inject into our consciousness moments of wonder, doubt, and self-analysis as to our real nature. Such moments, however, are occasional. Their intensity frightens us, and we tend to look away from what is exposed of ourselves. We develop in our lives complex warning systems and channels of escape from confrontations with reality. We go for the substitutes. Material objectives easily lull us into a basic satisfaction with, and therefore desire for, their gratification. To confront the people of God with ultimate realities is one of the Church's functions. Without confrontation there is no choice; without choice there can be no freedom. This is true in the moral and spiritual orders as well as in the material.

Contemporary man is inundated with advertised alternatives to facing reality in every area of his life. The nature of moral choice still remains deciding between good and evil, however. The choice we make ultimately leads to our enslavement or to our freedom. The Church's responsibility is to show forth freedom as the basis of unity, of the individual spirit or personality, or of social or international peace. The search for one's identity implies the possession of the freedom to perceive when the search is over. To accept the real "who" of oneself involves very considerable freedom.

Surely the Church has *something* to offer those who, in their confusion, seek freedom in psychedelic experiences or through other forms of contracting-out of a meaningless world. Much drug-taking involves the desire for a mystical experience of God, the breakthrough into a meaningful world which will not look like this one does, fragmented and sick unto death. Because of the uncertainty of her own priorities, the Church has failed to show what freedom means in practice. Because of our own disunity, Christians cannot demonstrate what a joyful thing it is for brethren to live together in unity. We do not look like a benevolent fraternity ourselves in either Church history or contemporary bickering over Church structure. The rejection of the Church by the many who search for a religious substitute could give us some very practical clues as to what the Church should reject about herself.

An intense period of re-evaluation and self-examination by many in the Church is getting well under way now. The *Honest to God* debate is one exciting example of attempted clarification of what we believe, in order to free the Christian to act validly. We can anticipate that such debate will increase as Christians are prepared to discard the optional extras in the search for the essentials of faith. Today, the volume of fragmentation in the world gives to the Church a unique opportunity to show what the peace of God is like in practice. But first, she must experience that peace herself.

What must be the agonized searchings of a Bishop Pike for truths through which he can live are symptoms not of faithlessness but of widespread rebellion against rigidity and formalism. Whatever may be the reaction of those who find that credal orthodoxy fully and adequately expresses their belief, Bishop Pike and others have shown that the "time for Christian candor" is long overdue.

> There are many people within the fold who have not really grasped the heart of the Christian message because they are bogged down by too many doctrines, mores, precepts, customs, symbols and other traditions, with no sense of differentiation between the relative essentiality and non-essentiality of the respective items.[1]

The enormous commercial success of the *Honest to God* type of book, and the public participation in the controversies that surround Bishop Pike, demonstrate far more than casual interest. The reception given to books such as Monica Furlong's *With Love to the Church*,[2] Pierre Berton's *The Comfortable Pew*,[3] and *God's Frozen People*[4] by Mark Gibbs and T. Ralph Morton, says a great deal about the response produced when the Church is prepared honestly to be self-critical.

From Rome to Canterbury, and just about at all points in between and beyond, so-called Christendom is in a ferment of theological and structural reappraisal. If attention paid by mass

---

[1]Pike, James A., *A Time for Christian Candor,* Harper & Row, New York, 1964, page 7.
[2]Hodder & Stoughton, London, 1965, Forward Movement Miniature Books, Cincinnati, Ohio, 1968.
[3]McClelland & Stewart, Toronto, and J. B. Lippincott Company, Philadelphia, 1965.
[4]Fontana Books, London, 1964, and Westminster Press, Philadelphia, 1965.

circulation magazines to such ecclesiastical "happenings" is anything to go by, they are observed with as much interest by the unchurched as by the faithful. For interest and attention, Christianity seems still to have an inside track whenever the Church indicates that she is in the race! Such an observation is bound to produce a verbal backlash, such as: "How dare it be suggested that the Church live by the popularity polls?" Agreed—but if she is not willing to accept the gauge of public interest as a help to effective communication, then, so far as preaching the Gospel to all nations is concerned, the Christian Church can pull down the shutters and close up the shop!

It is a long time since Christian doctrine or its exponents were subjects for living-room conversation! My own theological position is not always that of Bishop Pike, but there can be no doubt that he has become an apostle to the unchurched. Undoubtedly, he has caused problems to many who are "churched," and, as a result, *some* have joined the ranks of the unchurched. Partly, this is because Church members are not often challenged to do more than merely mouth credal truths. When the creeds go cold through the inaction of merely verbal recitation, then there is small wonder that they seem to lose their meaning. When the creeds are lived out, then the great and mighty truths they seek to express become understood because they are experienced. The inadequacy of human language does not then become confused with the truth of what we seek to describe. One suspects also that Christian living is no longer exclusively identified with Church membership.

The Trinity, for instance, to many Christians is a fact of experience. I simply cannot jettison my own understanding of God which coincides with, and no doubt has been conditioned by, that of Christians down the ages. The Virgin Birth, on the other hand, is of a totally different order of belief. Through the centuries, the virginity of Mary has been accepted. Historicity, however, and the validity of actual experience of the threefold persons of the one God in trinity, are of a totally different order of "proof." The words, "born of the Virgin Mary," state a historical consensus of accepted opinion at the time they were written. I can hardly experience Mary's virginity.

Scholarship, itself a means of revelation, can and should cause us to re-evaluate what has been treated as historical fact in the past. Venerable though a tradition may be, if doubt is raised as to its authenticity then the validity of the doubt must be assessed. A spirit of inquiry should be encouraged. The doctrine of the Trinity, however, is an attempt to define the consensus of continuing Christian experience from its formation. The validity of any Church doctrine surely does not depend on the accuracy of its formulation. What does matter is whether the doctrine, for example of the Trinity, expresses a truth today about the nature of God. Does what the Church teaches assist the Christian to say, "My own imperfect experience of God is explained by the verbal division of a God who in totality I cannot even begin to understand, but who, in His constituent parts, I can at least recognize?"

Bishop Pike has done the whole Christian Church a great service in sharing his difficulties with the world. He has removed the creeds from the torpor of familiarity. He has waxed hot or cold depending upon the stance of those who judge him. Certainly the last thing that can be said is that he has produced a tepid reaction from the Church at large. How much the specter of heresy trials reflects the personality problems of those who seek them rather than doctrinal differences is a matter of fascinating, psychological investigation. Bishop Pike is a maverick who has challenged both the Church's doctrine and her order. When the dust has settled on talk about heresy trials, perhaps we shall see that the main issue was that of Church order and not of doctrine at all. For the most part, we bishops are much more learned in matters affecting our jurisdiction than in theological debate. Church order is a sensitive point with those who stand to lose the most from doubts cast upon its eternal validity or infallible truth. Jim Pike has certainly touched some exposed nerves. The world, unfortunately, heard the screams and was not impressed by the quality of the pain!

My own need is to speak to the tremendous dissatisfaction I feel with the structure of the Church, as passionately as the exponents of the new theology speak of their dissatisfaction with finality in the forms of credal expression. It is in the light of my own acceptance, within my understanding, of most basic, orthodox, catholic, theological positions that I find myself increasingly concerned about the existing structures and priorities of the Church. The doctrine of the Church as the body of Christ creates an expectancy which simply is not realized by the Church as I know her. The doctrine of creation tells us much about the purpose of life and the world we live in. Those concerns with which the Church increasingly is occupied hardly reflect such priorities. We have become an inward-looking community, if indeed we can use the word "community" to describe the Church. Christians have become so parochial in their concerns that in practice they scarcely look beyond their own denominational horizons. It is small wonder, therefore, that we do not show to the world our capacity, indeed our vocation, to transcend our humanity in our quest for union with God. Theological orthodoxy demands discontent with the quality of the corporate expression of Christian life.

The prolific output of words on credal difficulties in a very real sense is a yardstick by which we can measure the difficulties of expressing intangible truths. Also, our controversies indicate a cause of our failure to communicate Christian truths to others who have not yet experienced them, or to those who have lost the faith in Christ which they once had. Is not another cause of this failure the inability of the institutional Church to speak to a world which is educated far and away beyond that of the time at which the truths were formulated? Infallibility and dogma are no longer the escape hatches of our uncertainties. Rigid explanations of living truth have greatly inhibited inquiries into the content of our faith. If those on the "inside" find the situation intolerable, we can hardly convince others that we have found all the answers. Blunted truths will not penetrate a toughened world. Dialogue not dogma is the vehicle of communicating truth today. Doctrinal truth which can be related to experience and therefore accepted and lived is eagerly sought by contemporary youth. Who can blame them if, in presentation or in application to life, the Church's doctrines are made to seem phony, dull, and unrelated to a fast changing world?

Man has transcended his physical environment. His moral capacity to handle the discoveries of science is a vastly different matter. It is time that the Church elevates her spiritual sights to see man where he really is—heaven-bent, but bound to an earth on which he still must learn to live.

III

WHY CAN'T THE CHURCH STICK TO RELIGION?

ANY CLERGYMAN who has ever emerged from his sanctuary to speak on social issues to the world outside will have been greeted, at some time or another, with the question, "Why can't the Church stick to religion?" This is a question thrown at the Church wherever the Church has indicated that she is not content to be a museum of ideas with the clergy as guides and curators.

In many parts of the United States, the Church's failure to give an articulate answer to this question has caught her in a cleft stick. On the one hand, there are those who are crying out for a Christ who has been released from the sanctuary and allowed to have a meaningful interaction with the profound concerns of the world. On the other hand, many a pledge has been cancelled because of what has seemed to be an uncomfortable and unwarrantable intrusion by the Church into the purely secular arena of social concerns.

In Britain, the Church's political pronouncements do not evoke the same degree of shock as elsewhere. Partly, this is because of the established position of the Church which gives to some of its bishops the political platform of the House of Lords. It is also because the interaction of Church and state over the centuries has created a society in which separation of Church and state in the American sense would be historically anomalous. Consequently, one of the greatest challenges facing the Church of England today is to be taken seriously enough by the people for them even to hear its social and political pronouncements, often of considerable worth and importance. Stuffy remoteness of all too many professional churchmen, coupled with an unfavorable image of the establishment, have shrouded with a boredom as heavy as London's fog the Church's attempts to "get with it." Many young and vitally concerned Christians in England are acutely aware that they have inherited a very outmoded structure of the Church. Many despair of ever effecting change; still more are deflected from the full-time ministry, and who can blame them? The Church of England has its fair share of talent and vision, especially among its younger clergy, but many of them are frustrated and feel trapped within a system that withers their vitality.

It is very difficult indeed for a bishop living in a "palace"—however the actual living conditions contrast with the popular idea—to identify with the remnant of the churched, let alone the vast mass of the unchurched. The extraordinary fact is that where a bishop does incur resentment by speaking to political or social issues, it is often because it is felt that the very political position he occupies should not be used. As merely a part of the decor of traditionalism which allows the House of Lords to survive at all in one of the most truly democratic societies in the world, the "Lord Bishop" invokes a sentimental toleration. When, however, his observations project Christian involvement in the world beyond noting the appearance of the first cuckoo in Spring, almost instinctive blocks are quickly brought into play. The soporific effect of long familiarity works to produce disregard, if not contempt. It is difficult, of course, for a bishop possessing the title of "Lord Bishop" and referred to as "My Lord" to overcome the connotation of secular aristocracy, which effectively removes the leaders of the Church from identification with the problems and concerns of the ordinary man. However jolly his lordship might try to be, as indeed many are, the public image of his status is devastating to effective communication.

Social levels, in which the Church is stratified near the top, leave little room to convince the ordinary layman that he is not excluded. This situation presents an urgent challenge to the English Church which is somewhat different from that presented to the Church in most other countries. If I speak with feeling, it is because in South Africa, where, even more than in England, medieval titles are used and certainly not generally discouraged, some of the bishops suffer from the isolating effect of anachronistic forms of address.

Identification, real or imaginary, with the privileges of outmoded aristocracy, must surely be seen as a tremendous hindrance to the Church's vocation to preach the Gospel. Translated into modern idiom, this has become the problem of communication. All too often, the Church seems to be so much a part of the establishment that an alert and inquisitive generation rejects its "non-religious" utterances as *ultra vires*. They are seen as part of the unwanted baggage of a society desperately trying to find its place in a world in which "the establishment" and all it connotates has little place. The world of gaiters, frock coats, rosebudded hats, and purple-clad milords, is far removed from the serious concern of anything but the theater. Ears today are attuned to the sound of the Beatles and their often authentic message. "Swinging London" and the Liverpool beat look for their expression to discotheque or disc. The tailors of Carnaby Street may have brought up to date Edwardian dress, but they certainly have not resurrected the way of life which it clothed.

The publication by a bishop's wife of a sadly entertaining book entitled, *Bishop's Wife But Still Myself*,[1] is obviously intended to reassure the world which may doubt that such a feat is possible. Perhaps nobody would ever have considered the reassurance necessary, but the title, used in all seriousness, raises unfortunate implications of how the Church looks at herself, and here is the heart of the problem.

Neither in the United States nor in South Africa has the Church any inbuilt and established right of social pronouncement. To be heard, she has to command an audience. There is no prefabricated constituency. Her right to speak is frequently challenged whenever concern is expressed for what the secular world regards as its prerogatives.

In South Africa the government itself is the chief poser of the question, "Why can't the Church stick to religion?" The role of religion as the upholder of the status quo, as it is often implied by government officials, is certainly not one which the Church can accept. The unmasking of "political bishops" is frequently the zealously pursued mission of cabinet ministers. Appropriately of late, in view of several deportation orders served on Anglican priests in South Africa, the chief spokesman on "political bishops" and their evils has been the Minister of Transport. A bishop becomes political in South Africa when, by anything he says or does, he opposes the ideology of apartheid by which South Africa is governed. Such opposition is interpreted as proof that he is a Communist, or at least a tool of the Communist conspiracy.

In most countries, the attempt to decrease the volume of human suffering and misery created by racism would be considered at least an accepted, if inconvenient, function of the

---

[1]Williams, Cicely, *Bishop's Wife But Still Myself,* George Allen & Unwin, Ltd., London, 1961.

Church. Not so in South Africa, however. The deportation of clergy and the refusal to grant entry visas to those who may be politically suspect, indicate some of the consequences of what the government thinks is the function of religion.

The Church in South Africa is becoming increasingly limited in the ability to express what she considers her vocation to be. The absence of any civil-rights movement in a situation which screams out for one to be developed reflects the enormous gap between what the Church says she is, and what her white members accept and would like her to be. The fact that so many white South Africans are leaving the Anglican Church for more comfortable pews raises disconcerting speculations. If it is increasingly difficult for the Church's *words* on race relations to be accepted by her white members, the practical application of the social gospel in an action program would be far reaching indeed. The dangers of inaction to the life of the Church seem to be far more pronounced, however, than anything she says or seems likely to do.

In the United States, there have been many drop-outs along the civil-rights road which many Christian churches have taken. Yet, at the same time, a strong remnant is emerging. Many members have been lost by all denominations active in the struggle for freedom. As many congregations are now finding, out of those people who remain can be created a strong and concerned core around which a stronger Christian community than existed before can be built. The challenge facing the Church is to help such new communities into an awareness that outreach not only follows survival—it is a prerequisite of the Christian life.

In South Africa there have been many impeccable ecclesiastical pronouncements on the dignity of man. What is sadly lacking is an action program to give to any remnant that survives something worth working for. It almost seems that the

Christian Church in South Africa has abandoned initiative in helping shape a new society. The Church in the United States is fighting desperately to gain such initiative. Maybe even there it is too late in the day, but the Christian Church at least is making the attempt, and, as a result, is deeply and increasingly involved in social issues. In South Africa the situation demands a Christian action program based on the mighty truth that Christ walks and not only talks, in His Father's world.

What a difference there is between action and reaction. To act involves the ability to seize initiative in a situation which demands it. To react involves a response to initiative taken elsewhere. This is largely the impression given by the Christian Church in South Africa: the response of verbal *reaction*.

Such reflex action of defensive and often outmoded retreat into pietism can be listed among the prime reasons why the African people do not look to the Church for their deliverance. They do not hear any Moses demanding, "Let my people go." There seems to be no leader to take them anywhere out of their misery and degradation. The black African has been obliged to live with hopelessness too long in South Africa, and his position worsens all the time. Maybe he understands far more about what Christian hope really is than the white man will ever know. The Church thinks that she has the market in faith and charity, but hope she does not even pretend to communicate. The sure and certain hope of a fuller life than this earthly existence has provided, gives to the black African a joyfulness and patience which never ceases to amaze the observer. It is so easy to use his joy and patience to hold him down. Faith and charity, in the sense of the profoundest love of which man is capable, precludes that possibility. It compels us to remove injustice, intolerance, and oppression.

If the institutional Church in South Africa will absorb into her withered bones the living hope of our non-white African brothers, then maybe the doctrine of Christian hope will come alive again. When that happens, there will be hope for the Church. It will have a more militant quality, however, than our otherworldliness might lead us to expect.

It is hardly surprising that the Church today looks rather like a tired, old actor searching for a part. There is a temptation to dwell nostalgically upon a past in which the institutional Church occupied center stage in history's leading role, certainly in the western world.

If we turn back a few pages of our history books, the Church's position in society was easily accepted because there was no alternative. It was the Church which took care of the poor; today, it is the welfare state in different national forms. A few chapters ago, it was the Church which ran the hospitals; today, Medicare in America, or the National Health Service in England provides care for the sick. Even where government has not taken over, the practice of medicine is jealously guarded by private and professional interests. Today, the Church's hospitals in most parts of the world certainly are not the primary source of healing. In many parts of Africa, where Christian hospitals are still sometimes the mainstay of medicine, one gains some idea of what Europe would have shown several hundreds of years ago. Increasingly, however, government is either taking over or financing even these African remnants of the Church's concern for the body of man.

Then we look at education. A few chapters back in history the Church just about had a monopoly in literacy. Many of the great universities and schools were religious foundations. To provide education today is by no means the prerogative of the Church. Look where we will, politics, economics, art, and music, all have passed far and away beyond the Church's capacity to decisively influence. Even the confessional has been replaced by the couch for the majority of those who seek relief from the pain of guilt. The monastic house, or its parochial successor, simply cannot cope as the dispenser of education and medicine together with alms for relief of body, mind, and soul. The state with all of its resources can perform most of these functions much more effectively. The Church's job is to help the specialists by showing and teaching what it means to be the inheritors of what once were the Church's major concerns. The real task now is to get across that both specialists and their clientele are in fact the Church. Together they are the people of God.

It is easy for us to forget that a few chapters in the history book represents an era of massive revolution. Over the surging tide of new ideas the Church has lost control. It is much easier to turn back pages in a book than to turn back the effect of centuries which the pages represent. Here the comparison ends between the Church and the aging actor who takes sad refuge in the comfort provided by his fading clippings. It is futile to bemoan the Church's former glories, if glories they were. The Church today has an increasingly decisive role to play in the secular society. The Church must first establish her freedom to speak and act. She must be expansive in her acceptance of the fact that God's continued revelation of the purpose of creation is not limited by our professional sacred cows. Whether individually or in society, which all too easily we dismiss as "secular," man has developed and will continue to develop. The Church's job is to develop with him. Jesus Christ is in laboratory, civil rights movement, mental hospital, big business and slum. Where Christ is, the Church is, whether we see the body or not. Our task is to provide the hands, the eyes, the ears and feet of the body of Christ, giving to His ascended life and power an extended incarnation in our lives.

And so the question, "Why can't the Church stick to religion?" presents in its answer a tremendous teaching opportunity. It demands the discovery by the Church of the ever-changing role which she is called by God to play in the developing life of mankind. To "stick to religion" is to remain locked within her past. Also, it is to accept as her nature what society does not find difficult to tolerate. To stick to religion is to speak "comfortably," in the modern and debased sense of the word.

The civil-rights movement in the United States has compelled the Christian Church to take a stand. What should be a civil rights movement in South Africa, the land of apartheid, should compel the Christian Church there to show to the world our concern for the dignity of man. What could very well become the need for a civil-rights movement in Britain will soon compel the British Churches to take a stand. It is where the Gospel challenges the individual to transcend his selfishness and established pattern of life, that social involvement by the Church will most readily be criticised by those whose selfish interests are challenged. To "stick to religion" means to act on the Church's ultimate purpose; that is to reconcile man to God. This means that the theological basis in all areas of social action must be clearly defined.

At this point, a note of caution should be sounded. Of course, it is right for the Church to ally herself with civil-rights groups. If the cause is just, then the Church must help fight for it. The Christian, however, must be alive to the fact that the ticket bought by many "secular" civil-rights groups does not take us to the end of the line. If tomorrow the miracle were to occur, and man were able to live at peace with himself and with his brother, the work of the civil-rights groups would have been accomplished. Not so, however, the work of the Church. Her main task would remain to be completed, which is man's reconciliation with his God.

It is so easy for Christian people to become blinded to the

ultimate goal in our enthusiasm for the immediate objectives in which our humanity is involved. The offense of man's inhumanity to his brother, whether through racism or any other cause of degradation, is easy to feel. Properly, it evokes our response to remove the wrong. We wish to heal the pain to ourselves which such wrong causes, and to all its other victims, for wrong makes victims of us all.

There is not a similar sensitivity, however, to the consequences of man's rejection of God. The damage and corrosion caused to the world and its values by our rejection of God are not always apparent. What we must realize is that our journey is by no means over when brotherhood fills the neighborhood which the world has become. It must be taught and shown that without God man cannot fulfill the vast potential of his nature. It is in this direction that the Christian contribution most vitally can be made.

Peace on earth, good will among men is impossible until peace with God has been accomplished. When this concept is brought into the whole movement for civil rights, then the terms "black power," or "white power," will be seen as impoverished terms. "Black power" is a cry from the heart of South Africa, the United States, or wherever else men of color are denied justice and equal opportunities. The concept has its own inbuilt momentum and validity. When the cry is bitter, it reflects the frustration and disillusionment with the experienced alternative of white power. African power in Africa is a concept which, if it is not too late, the Church should help develop and articulate. The Christian community, consisting of both white and non-white, need not fall victim to the backlash of fear, feeding the desperation of which violent black power is born. What Christianity can offer is the awareness of the power of God, which, in the hands of men alive to its meaning, can be black, white, yellow, or brown. The power of God is the power of life and of love. Only such power can make of civil rights a true part of the human right to be divine. This is what is meant by man's creation in the image of God. Here is the thrust of our concern as Christians and, therefore, the battle line of the Church's engagement with the world. Still, the civil-rights movement remains an example of what the secular world would dearly like to exclude from religious involvement.

In South Africa, the pressures exerted on the white Christian to compromise are very great—the temptation to enjoy "the South African way of life" very real. This is why, to many of us, the doctrine of creation emerges as an anchor of sanity. It compels that the truth be spoken loud and clear, and it provides the supreme affirmation that because Christ is King we need not fear what man can do. The doctrine of creation generates its own source of courage.

It is when we apply the living out of what Christ means to the Christian that we run into trouble, because Christ cannot be contained within the framework of purely mental activity. He bursts out of the mental process into the physical consequences of our acceptance of Him. He becomes the whole within which all the divisions of life are a part. Thus, to the Christian, no part of the life of man can be seen outside the context of Christ's concern. Sticking strictly to religion, the Church can never accept any definition of her function which exempts from any part of the whole life of man the redemptive power of Jesus Christ. To do so would be to deny the sovereignty of God over the totality of His world. When we deny this, we deny our being. We die the death of people who, as James Baldwin has pointed out, when they treat people like things, become things themselves.

Running right through the purpose of man's existence is the idea of love—the love of self, the love of neighbor, the love of God. How, if I cannot love myself, can I love my neighbor when self is the yardstick by which I measure my love of others? If I cannot love the brother whom I have seen, then it is impossible for me to love the God whom I have not seen. In order to love, I must be free, because love cannot be compelled. If I am bigger and stronger and more powerful than you are I can compel most things, but not your love. To love myself, to love you my neighbor, to love my God, I must be free to reject. Freedom is the foundation of the virtue of loving because it permits a moral choice and involves an act of will. In order to love, I must be able and free to know whom and what I love. In the debased coinage of words, love has been devalued to the point where it can refer in intensity as much to candies and movies as to human beings.

When we say that in apartheid or any racist legislation, my ability to know my neighbor is diminished, we are expressing a religious consequence of political action. My ability to love my neighbor is diminished to the degree of the separation which is legislated. This is a religious consequence too, because it profoundly affects my ability to fulfill the purpose of my creation.

If the separation is the *de jure* legislation of a Mississippi or a South Africa, then the Church becomes involved in a direct confrontation with the state, because the state is transcending its legitimate authority. The Church cannot give to Caesar the things that belong to God. To know my neighbor in order to love him is my responsibility for which I, not the state, must give account.

If the separation is *de facto*, as in housing discrimination in the northern United States, or as in many parts of Britain, then again the Church must speak and act. To do so will be out of love and concern for those who discriminate as well as for those who are their victims. Fair-housing programs and legislation must be actively supported by individual Christians and by organized Church groups. It is not enough merely to preach about the brotherhood of man. Christians must show what the doctrine of brotherhood means in practice. To help remove *de facto* segregation wherever it is found is a very good place for Christians to start. As often as not we will begin within ourselves.

To remain silent where either *de jure* or *de facto* segregation exists is the abrogation of the Church's nature. When such silence occurs, then the Church has ceased to be "religious."

If the Church goes where the pain is, and shows to the world that Christ can remove the pain where it really hurts, then Christian credentials are seen to be good. We must take a hard look at some of the areas of pain in which the healing power of Christ can be applied. To do more than just look at them will require drastic surgery on the Church herself before, in her own wholeness, she can strike a responsive chord in the yearning of man to be whole. Only when she has become what she herself lays claim to be can she speak to the contemporary condition of man in isolation from himself, his brother, and his God.

When the Church's identity has become established and manifest, to be called a "political bishop" will no longer be a slur. The question, "Why can't the Church stick to religion?" will be answered by society itself. The boundaries of sacred and secular will have merged. When the Church has liberated herself, she will be free to be the Body of Christ, and once again man, wherever and whatever he may be, will be able to see what he can become by becoming one with Christ.

IV

HOW TO SUCCEED IN BUSINESS WITHOUT REALLY DYING

THE PHRASE, "Mutual Responsibility and Interdependence in the Body of Christ," so far as the Anglican Communion is concerned, is the child of the Toronto Congress of 1963. It became the title of a program designed to give a much-needed face lift to Anglicanism. M.R.I., as the cumbersome title became abbreviated, was seen almost as a magic formula to create instant communion.

Many Anglicans are not aware, however, that the attempt to discover the meaning of mutual responsibility in the wider Christian fellowship is by no means new. In the first instance, the concept of interdependence was expressed through overseas missions, and mutual responsibility was seen in missionary or "sending" terms.

After World War II, as the result of massive and obvious needs, there was a growth of perception as to what mutual care really involved. Mutual responsibility was seen in the stark reality of caring for the tragic refuse of man's greed for human life. The number of refugees and displaced persons throughout Europe demanded that Christian concern be expressed in terms of immediate outreach. There was no time to theorize. Expansion of the idea of interdependence from the old missionary sense of providing education and hospitals for the heathen, to the responsibility of Christians one for another, followed inevitably.

The real breakthrough on the world Christian scene came about the time of the Second Assembly of the World Council of Churches in Evanston, Illinois, in 1954, when inter-church aid was seen much more in terms of general human need rather than of specific Christian affiliation.

By 1961, at New Delhi, the World Council of Churches had developed a position which emphasized mutual responsibility in terms of service to the world as well as service to churches and special need.

> 77. It is rather easy to make an idealistic and abstract appraisal of Christian service. It is not difficult to criticize the limitations of the current forms of service such as hospitals and educational institutions. But our task is to engage in positive participation and concrete involvement in search for the forms of Christian service in the contemporary world which meet real and deep needs. This requires a constant effort to open ourselves to the calling of Christ to serve the world and to commit ourselves to respond humbly yet courageously to his suffering ministry in all realms of life, together with the whole Church of Jesus Christ.[1]

Thus, the dimension of Christian service to which the whole Christian community must witness became dramatically enlarged. Service received a two-dimensional aspect. The mutuality of our interdependence and responsibility within the Christian community was acknowledged; secondly, Christian service took its place within the larger framework of the brotherhood of man regardless of religious affiliation.

The *New Delhi Report* of the Third Assembly of the World

---

[1]*New Delhi Report,* The Third Assembly of the World Council of Churches, 1961, S.C.M. Press, London, 1962, page 111.

Council of Churches is a salutary reminder to Anglicans that to coin a phrase does not give any monopoly of its underlying principles. The program, Mutual Responsibility and Interdependence in the Body of Christ, as adopted at the Anglican Congress in Toronto, 1963, in fact gave expression to only one level of mutuality, limited as it was to Anglicanism. The wise words spoken at the Congress by the Archibishop of Canterbury, presiding at the Anglican baptism of M.R.I., were well received at the time: "The Church that lives to itself will die by itself." These words, applied to the whole Christian community, find a broad base in what had previously emerged from New Delhi in 1961.

> 88. . . . ecumenical demonstrations of inter-church aid are needed and they should be shared by all churches regardless of denominational allegiances. The static distinction of 're-ceiving church' and 'giving church' must go so that all will share spiritual, material and personal gifts in the light of the total economy of the household of God.[2]

It is against this background that we look at M.R.I., and I ask non-Anglican readers to make the translation to the programs and situations in their own communions.

However behind the times its limited operations may have been, for Anglicans the concept of mutual responsibility and interdependence soared beyond the trifles with which the religious professionals had become absorbed. We were to raise our sights to take in the broad vista of the Anglican Church as a Communion. The needs of any one part were to become the needs of the whole. Just as when there is pain in any one part, the whole body feels it and is affected by it, so the pain of the Church would be felt by the whole. Acceptance of even the narrow, denominational concept of M.R.I. by the Anglican

---

[2]*Ibid.*, p. 113. *New Delhi Report*, The Third Assembly of the World Council of Churches, 1961, S.C.M. Press, London, 1962.

Congress in Toronto was one of the most significant break-throughs which the Church had experienced in a long time. Acceptance of the theory provided the opportunity for the Church to act as a communion.

M.R.I. marks the opening of the doors of the Church to allow one aspect of the doctrine of creation, for so long contained within the institution, to flood the world in expressing our concern for each other. In our mutuality and interdependence we reflect the unity of God's creation, the unity of man's salvation in Jesus Christ.

It was refreshing to read affirmation of this truth by the Executive Secretary of the Overseas Mission Society of the Episcopal Church, in his excellent book, *Christian Responsibility in One World*.[3] The book makes invaluable reading for those who wish to raise their sights above local and parochial concerns. It places our Christian response in world perspective.

"Where does our motivation come from now?" Mr. Eastman asks, after pleading for a new theology of world mission.

> It comes in fact from a clear understanding of who God is, what His will is for the world, how He takes initiative in redeeming the world, and what role in the history of salvation he has assigned to the Church. It comes in part from the willingness of Christian men individually and the Church corporately to be open to the wind of the Holy Spirit as it blows across our world. To declare that "the Church exists to witness, to obey, and to serve," is not enough. Ways must be found to engender faithful and eager obedience to our calling without the defects of fear, self-satisfaction, or grudging compliance. Such is the basic and difficult challenge of mutual responsibility and interdependence. That is why the theological problem is really the key to the entire effort."[4]

---

[3]Eastman, A. Theodore, *Christian Responsibility in One World,* The Seabury Press, Inc., New York, 1965.
[4]*Ibid.,* p. 95.

I have quoted at length from Mr. Eastman's book because my own concern for the theological priorities of our task is affirmed and emphasized by an Anglican whose own experience of the problem of contemporary mission is reflected on every page. The fact that the Overseas Mission Society is not one of the best known and best supported societies in the Episcopal Church in the United States reflects the struggle for mission, in the widest sense of the word, to be recognized as the Church's *raison d'être*.

In M.R.I., the Anglican Church has taken the plunge, and it is a deep plunge. To go back now would be fatal. It would be to proclaim by default our blindness to the constantly developing vision of the direction which we must follow.

But M.R.I. has run into trouble—serious trouble. Perhaps as a concept it is a child born out of due time. Already there has been a cutback from original expectations. It has been found necessary to adopt more realistic appraisals of what interdependence in theory should produce of mutuality in practice. Much more teaching at the congregational level was necessary before the revolutionary idea conceived at the top could be followed through. Merely to say that people do not give generously enough is to miss the spirit of M.R.I. Such oversimplification, furthermore, evades the real question of why it is falling short of what was hoped would result. There seem to be two big problems crying for attention.

The first problem is clearly that of not having plowed the ground before the seed was planted. M.R.I. presents a world vision of the communion of the Church in community. The same seed was scattered over the whole ground at the same time. The enlivening ideal of mission, which M.R.I. presupposes, finds its most fertile ground where stewardship has been taught and practised, however far from our goals even the best practice of stewardship might be. There is a vast difference, however, between the various parts of the Anglican Church in their acceptance of the meaning of Christian stewardship.

In the American and Canadian churches Christian stewardship has become a refined and, on the whole, basically accepted witness to faith in the trusteeship of material possessions. The same sense of trusteeship of time and talents, although more widely and better taught in the United States and Canada than anywhere else in the Anglican Church, has received nowhere near the attention as that given to the stewardship of money. Obviously, no true doctrine of Christian stewardship can exempt time and talent from the demands of trusteeship.

In Britain, although financial stewardship is being taught and practised increasingly, Eric James has pointed out that in her dependence upon endowments, the English Church relies more upon the dead than upon the living! In a letter to the *Church Times*,[5] Canon James commented on a speech made by the Bishop of Woolwich in the Church Assembly in February, 1965, in which he criticized the Church's failure to think radically, as invited by Toronto. Canon James wrote:

> Further thought and examination leads me to these conclusions:
>
>   1. The Church Commissioners' grant for stipends in the year to 31st March, 1964, was £11,450,452. Of this figure, *dead* Christians provided £10,949,707, *live* Christians £500,745, i.e., 4.4%. Friends who serve the Church overseas tell me that the proportion of what the dead and the live give in the Church overseas is at a rough guess the reverse of this.
>
> I believe now that the Church of England is not beginning to fulfill its obligations under Mutual Responsibility and In-

---

[5]Issue of March 12, 1965.

terdependence until it is giving away most if not all of this annual subsidy of £11 million from the graveyards.

He further asks the question:

> And would not the withdrawal of this money force us to make an "agonizing re-appraisal" of many other aspects of our work—upkeep of buildings, full time staff, etc.? My experience is that often only finance forces people to face theological questions.
>
> 2. *Dead* Christians, through the Church Commissioners, relieved the living Church in England of the need to find £1,255,137 towards the cost of new or repaired buildings during the same period. . . .
>
> Is it not time that we took action to tithe—at least—our receipts from *dead* Christians for the benefit of the living Church overseas? . . . In other words, how long are our policies at home and in relation to the Church overseas going to be cushioned by the financial establishment?

Eric James, now Canon of Southwark Cathedral, adds sorrowfully, "But no bishop says anything like this publicly."

As for most other branches of the Anglican Communion, stewardship of money has a long way to go before the forward thrust of M.R.I. can be attained in practice. What certainly applies to South Africa is relevant to most Anglican dioceses outside the United States and Canada, and still to a large degree to Britain.

A recent systematic and professional study, on which it is hoped to base a more dynamic approach to Christian giving, shows that in South Africa in one of the wealthiest dioceses—Natal—slightly over one half of 1 per cent of "Anglican" income is given to the Church. In two other dioceses, Johannesburg and Cape Town, the percentage is a mere .38 of 1 per cent and .37 of 1 per cent respectively. In some of the poorer dioceses, such as Kimberley and Kuruman, the figure is just short of 1 per cent. The diocese of George shows the highest percentage of Anglican income being given to the Church. The figure is a little over 2 per cent.

The reason for this pathetic standard of giving is, of course, a long standing failure to teach Christian stewardship in any wider context than that of housekeeping, or "paying our bills." When we take a general look at Anglican stewardship in practice, it is like unearthing a foundation stone of an ancient building in which has been placed for posterity's interest a few coins of the time!

And so a massive program of education is urgently needed, geared to the widely different level of existing awareness of what Christian stewardship really means in terms of time, talent, and material resources. If the already abridged M.R.I. targets are to be attained, let alone developed and expanded in future years, such a policy is essential. It must be initiated at the top and designed for easy assimilation by the parishes. Such a program might well be a top candidate for inclusion on the agenda of the next Anglican Congress. Its initial purpose would be to even up the ground throughout the Church, in terms of the development of Christian stewardship. The American and Canadian Churches would have a considerable responsibility here in sharing their experience with churches less advanced in concepts and, let's face it, techniques of planned giving.

A co-ordinated educational program throughout the Anglican Communion is needed urgently, applied with sensitivity to local needs and conditions. Stewardship would have to be placed in the arena of mission and its challenge. The training of selected personnel would create problems but would be essential. Many of the poor dioceses, perhaps, would have to make do with regional or provincial directors of Christian stewardship. Many other dioceses, not so poor, would train and employ their own specialists. Even in a diocese as far removed from outside social or ecclesiastical influence as is Kimberley, there is now a full time Director of Christian Stewardship. But the ground had first to be well and truly laid by the bishop personally leading stewardship missions in every parish and mission in the 150,000-square-mile diocese. American readers cannot really be aware of how backward is the practice of planned giving outside the United States and Canada. Many American and Canadian bishops are filled with righteous indignation at the often poor level of stewardship in their dioceses, but if they were to inherit the level of giving in South Africa they would, I think, change their tune!

The price of the lack of earlier and systematic preparation is now becoming apparent. All of this is an attempt to face up to a prime reason why M.R.I. has faltered at the ordinary parish level; why it now lacks the fire of the vision it had at its inception; and why it smacks of a gimmick. To the man in the pew it looks suspiciously like an attempt to internationalize his pledge for the Church's foreign aid program.

If M.R.I. is ultimately a theological truth in practice, the theological truth must be taught, and taught quickly, before we lose sight entirely of the opportunity for emancipation which it offers. It is not a threat to anything but selfish independence and irresponsibility. Such a threat must become a challenge. Lack of initial preliminary preparation already has cost us dear. If we do not act now, it could cost us our freedom to be truly the Church. A vision received and lost, like a "conversion experience," is hard to come by again.

In practice, M.R.I. seems to have become bogged down and the men and women who administer it are fighting to give it life and meaning. But the very atmosphere of the Church is against them. M.R.I. could well become the victim of the system, unless the vision of those who conceived it, and now seek to operate it, is given a chance for creative expression. The infant mortality rate of good ideas in the Church runs very high.

The second problem which has to be tackled is one increasingly met when the Church becomes efficient. It is a problem which we have inherited in our attempt to show the world that we too can use computers. The problem is to obtain the balance between planned efficiency and generated spontaneity in the establishment of true priorities.

If I feel passionately about this, it is because I speak out of what used to be called a missionary situation in the days when a missionary was thought of as being a minister, preferably with an English accent, reading Bible stories to grateful natives seated under trees. Now I speak out of what is called a "receiving Church."

We have built out of the people of God an administrative monster. Into this monster, M.R.I. has been fed and, like so many other of God's gifts, is likely to be devoured. I believe it is true to say that, if the administrative work of the Church were to be cut by 50 per cent today, the Kingdom of God would not be delayed one minute tomorrow. It might even be advanced, if the vocation to serve people and to meet their deepest needs was not swallowed up increasingly in the need to keep running the machinery we have built.

I say this because the doctrine of creation tells me that this is God's world. The doctrine of the Church tells me enough about her purpose to know that we are the servants and not the masters of God or His people. M.R.I. is our opportunity to live out the fast-fading awareness of vocation of the People of God to be a servant Church. It is our opportunity to achieve the drastic change in direction so desperately needed, if we are to move with the winds of change and cease to drift aimlessly.

There is an increasing awareness that M.R.I.'s reputation needs to be rescued from the administrator's desk. Having had

some personal experience of the tremendous concern, outreach, and sheer talent of those who administer M.R.I. in the
Overseas Department of Executive Council in New York, I
know how way off the mark their image is. To bridge the gap
between what a considerable number of people think M.R.I.
has become, and what those who are trying to administer it
long and work for it to be, requires a public relations job of
considerable magnitude in the United States and elsewhere.
Almost everywhere resistance to centralized control of overseas giving is now encountered. Sometimes the resistance reflects unjustified contentment with the status quo and is in fact
the resistance of convenience. But there is a very real danger
of depersonalizing something which is very personal.

To give because we are led to respond to needs outside ourselves can and should develop into planned giving. But there
is also a hidden stream of generosity in most of us which needs
to be reached by the sharp realization of other people's poverty, suffering, and needs. It is this stream which M.R.I. has to
tap at first in spontaneity, then consistently through the program of education suggested earlier. But even then, the spontaneity of generous response often well below the surface of
planned giving should not be administered out of existence.

Two suggestions may help in this regard. The first is obvious
and often made, but there is merit in it nevertheless. The cost
of administering M.R.I. must be kept to a minimum. This
applies particularly to the United States. I am sure that costs
are less than many institutional charities can boast, but there
is an undoubted and widespread discontent with what appears
to be an expensive front to the New York store. To remedy
this surely would not be an insuperable task.

Secondly, the matter of "preaching" tours by "missionary"
bishops in the United States, Canada, and other affluent societies must be handled sensitively and reasonably by both over-

seas bishops and by home dioceses and Executive Council. A preaching tour is one in which we hope that if money just should happen to be given for our work, this will reflect the excellence of our preaching and not the purpose of our tour! At one and the same time, such tours can be a plain nuisance and an embarrassment. If properly handled, they can also be an exciting and stimulating experience, both for overseas bishops and for those with whom they share their concerns and needs. Because of its affluence and generosity hardly equaled elsewhere, the United States is a sitting duck for a bishop overseas with an eye to quick capital gains! It would be a pity to see M.R.I. become one office of some ecclesiastical Department of Internal Revenue, but control there must be.

Much more creative use could be made of personal contact with overseas bishops and not just through companion-diocese programs and relationships. Much can be taught through personal contact about the real meaning of M.R.I. without asking for or being given any money at all. Yet, some overseas bishops and priests are proved crowd drawers—and, dare we say so, money raisers—and M.R.I. at the moment has need of some properly channeled box office appeal! The point is this, that personal contact with those who can trigger the spirit of generosity in expressed concern and Christian outreach, is one antidote to the dangers of remote control of the gigantic program we call M.R.I. In removing the old chaos and lack of discipline in giving outside ourselves, we must not let the baby go out with the old bath water.

At the root of our concern to establish a proper balance between spontaneity and the efficient handling of stewardship at depth is the need to retain perspective in priorities. The great opportunity which M.R.I. provides to the Church is to free real priorities from the dead weight of our entrenched parochialism. In this lies the Church's freedom to be herself.

V

FROM RAGS TO RICHES

WHEN WE LOOK at our ecclesiastical priorities, our hearts sink at an apparent incapacity to burst out of our preoccupation with ourselves. Endless debates as to whether an electric dishwasher should be provided for the parish kitchen or a new carpet for the church, divisive bickering and even schisms over parish fetes, are manifestations of our disease. There are millions of people in many dioceses who have no dishes to wash because they have nothing to eat from them. There are millions of Christians throughout the world whose parish project cannot be the provision of a carpet costing thousands of dollars, because they would have no church in which to put one. Fetes and bazaars in many parts of rural Africa would be difficult where currency means cattle, and where the main effort of life is to survive. There are inbuilt priorities in this life which are so easily obscured in the affluent society. This danger makes the Church's priorities all the more needful of clear evaluation and recognition. The Church must cure her own sickness which society all too clearly recognizes as being a reflection of its own before the Church can be the dispenser of the divine prescription to cure the ills of mankind.

Surely we can meet our basic needs in such a way as to assist others meet their own? I am not advocating for one minute that a mud or dung church, so often to be seen in many African dioceses, should be the symbol of the servant church in one of the prosperous cities in the U.S.A. or in Britain. What I am pleading for is that sense of mutual responsibility which says, "As long as there are people without any church, ours will be less expensive, so that when we build our church they can build one too."

I cannot see how, for instance, if the spirit of interdependence is to come alive, a church costing $100,000 can be afforded if the community building it cannot tithe 10 per cent for a church overseas. Recently, I was in a church in the United States which had just put down a carpet that cost far more than it would cost to build a church in my own diocese. Another had spent $75,000 on an organ, replacing an existing one which in most parts of the world would have been considered a prize, if not an extravagance. (All this five years after the M.R.I. charter of Toronto stated, "A new organ in Lagos or New York . . . might mean that twelve fewer priests are trained in Asia or Latin America.") Another church had spent over $100,000 on a parking lot for the extraordinary reason, to those of us whose people often walk miles on an empty stomach to worship God, that without close parking its parishioners would not come to church if they had to walk several blocks. Now this sort of spending is mutual irresponsibility and independence on a fantastic scale.

Personally, I believe that Jesus Christ would find Himself at home in our dung churches in the Kalahari Desert. More so, perhaps, than in many of the plush museum pieces of community status which so often mirror the reflected physical affluence of the surrounding society.

It is so easy to confuse the God whom we worship with the —

world's worship of itself, and often our churches provide the altar for this. In many parishes throughout the world, little is done to help people understand that the altars of our churches are not banquet tables where the King and His courtiers socialize in all their medieval trappings. At our altars we receive the food which strengthens us for our confrontation with a hostile or at best apathetic world. The altar looks outward to the world in which the people of God live, not inward to the peacock's tail of a Church satisfied with the way it looks in pretty sanctuaries and in comfortable pews!

Of course, there are rare exceptions, like oases in the desert, where people can drink and eat, and then resume their journey fortified, refreshed, and encouraged to go on. Such parishes are alive and demand a positive response to their existence from the surrounding community. They are engaged in the world and are alive to the multiplicity of men's needs. We need only read *Come Out The Wilderness*,[1] by Bruce Kenrick, to get some insight of what the Dean of New York's General Theological Seminary has called *New Patterns for Christian Action*.[2] In isolated pockets across the United States and in Britain, communities of dynamic Christians are to be found, probing incarnationally deep into surrounding life.

The comfortable myths which are used to explain lack of interest in church programs cannot be allowed to lull us into the acceptance of what we resignedly think is inevitable "these days." The real reason for apathy is the frequent absence of any meaningful program designed to meet the needs of the second half of the twentieth century. The beautifully ordered, candlelit world of the Church of well-pressed trouser knees, but shiny seats, does not illuminate the neglected wasteland

[1]Harper and Row, New York, and William Collins & Sons, London, 1962.
[2]Wylie, Samuel J., *New Patterns for Christian Action,* The Seabury Press, Inc., New York, 1959.

which TV is criticized for reflecting. In a chapter headed "The Church Irrelevant," Bruce Kenrick found a vital faith and a deep spirit of worship in the simple Harlem storefront churches "wedged in between the gin mills and candy stores and tumble-down Chinese laundries.[3] "In their simplicity," he writes, "they were an easy target for sophisticated critics."

Sophisticated critics are to be found in a sophisticated church, if by that is meant a streamlined and elegant showplace of canned joy in a crying, hungry and alienated world. I do not believe that Christ rejects beauty as seen in splendid buildings and facilities. On the contrary, I am sure that He expects us to provide the best we can for all His children to learn of Him, to worship Him, and to enjoy the fellowship of the brotherhood. I do believe, however, that He rejects priorities which place buildings above people, administration above the purpose of administration, means before ends. The doctrine of creation compels me to believe that what we make with our hands is subordinate to that made by God. We put the cart before the horse in the service we give to things. When the lines of priorities dictated by the physical needs of men are manifestly those involving starvation, illiteracy, persecution, and all its consequences, then the Church above those lines must measure all that it does by the needs of the Church below them. This is to be mutually responsible and interdependent in the body of Christ.

If, instead of yet another money-raising gimmick, M.R.I. were to be given the spirit of a life of mission in all the fullness of our new understanding of that word, then and then alone could it recover the impetus of its birth and be on the move. It is a great temptation for the bishop of a very poor overseas diocese to smack his lips with anticipation as to what his dio-

---

[3]Kenrick, Bruce, *op. cit.*, p. 27.

cese can get out of M.R.I. It is not only the failure to establish real and valid priorities in the Church in the affluent countries which has caused M.R.I. to be something of a damp squib. It is also the failure of dioceses in the poor societies to see it as anything more than another source of much-needed money, to which they need contribute nothing because, viewed solely in terms of material giving, they have nothing to offer.

As long as our giving to mission is seen merely as the savings bank of the Church where the poor can draw on the deposits of the wealthy, yet another great example of God's revelation of His will will receive an indeterminate sentence. Recent tours of the U.S.A. and of Britain have convinced me that we are ready to see beyond this if only we are taught.

For my own part, I see my visits home to the U.S.A. essentially as a contribution to the sense of interdependence. A diocese such as Kimberley and Kuruman can give little by way of financial support. We can and must do a great deal through our teaching of Christian stewardship to increase our self-support, and thereby release for others money from overseas upon which we have for so long depended. This we are trying to do. But so long as we pay our black African priests lower salaries, because they are black, than our white priests receive, we will continue to rationalize injustice by our poverty. Giving outside ourselves in such a case could put the respectable cloak of selflessness onto a socially accepted skeleton of gross selfishness and injustice. Mission means so much more than money. It demands a costly and often risky use of what we have. It would be easier for the average white-dominated Finance Committee in a South African diocese to contribute outside itself, than to take the obvious step of setting its own house in order by equalizing salaries paid to black and white priests. Not to do so is to present an extremely defective concept of the nature of the Christian ministry.

Kimberley and Kuruman, and similar diocese, can, should, and must give outside themselves in assisting to enlarge the total vision of what the Church is. This we can do by allowing the whole Church to share the perspective of our experiences and problems. In a very insignificant way, I dedicated my 1966 U.S. tour to this end, to make to the affluent Church an offering of the experience and life of a poor part of the body of Christ. The impact of the story of life in South Africa, and the agony of the Christian conscience in searching to know how it can be lived, was very considerable in the United States. It is a story of which people have heard and read many times, but of which some are almost totally ignorant.

In South Africa, the Christian Church is set in the midst of legislated white domination which in practice leads to gross inequalities and great suffering. Our 15 million non-white people have no vote, no direct representation in their government. They cannot live or work where they choose; they see very little hope of change. Economically depressed, their educational facilities are far below the standards provided for the white population of some 3½ million. The ever growing economic gap between whites and non-whites is the inevitable product of totally unequal opportunities. In such a situation our efforts to alleviate suffering of the deprived and, at the same time, to minister compassionately to those who directly or indirectly contribute to the social and spiritual malaise can offer a great deal to the wider Christian fellowship.

For many, however, the awareness of the struggle of the Church overseas to develop a truly confessional position in the midst of almost overwhelming obstacles, is enlivened by the physical contact with one who works there. And so my tour was an offering of perspective, a sharing of that concern which finds a response in our mutuality and interdependence.

During my tour I spoke of money, yes indeed, though not

merely to solicit gifts for our diocese. Rather, to give through the story of our poverty, a sense of proportion as to the right use of money in what by our standards is the affluent Church of the affluent society. Many individual churches in the United States have annual incomes far greater than the budget of the entire diocese of Kimberley and Kuruman, and this fact demands responsible awareness and response.

Many people gave to us spontaneously. The validity of this outreach convinced me that the administration of our mission program must beware that there is no stifling of spontaneity in response to needs made clear. Of course, there must be discipline in our giving and a comparable discipline in insuring that the needs of the Church are seen with each particular one taking its place in the whole. Never, however, should we inhibit or discourage spontaneous response through personal contact with those who are working in the field. Rather, should we seek to enliven such spontaneity among Christians, for spontaneity of worship, love or action is at a premium.

Then on my tour I spoke also of freedom. Not primarily to evoke sympathy for those who suffer the tragic consequences of its removal, but rather to enable people to appreciate the awesome responsibility and privilege of possessing freedom. I spoke of the spiritual wealth and depth of much of the Church's life in our materially poor diocese, not to boast but to show that poverty and hardship, inaccessibility and lack of Church facilities, do not necessarily lead to spiritual decline and neglect of the heart of the Christian life.

The materially poor dioceses have a great deal to offer to the materially rich ones. In many ways the task is more straightforward. Perhaps the very absence of any capacity to feed the administrative monster which the Church so often makes of herself is the key to the liberation of the Church in many parts of the world. We cannot afford the luxury of preoccupation with buildings, machines, and things, because we possess so few of them. In our poverty, though, we do have something to offer, and in mutual responsibility and interdependence we must offer it. Then, the affluent churches must be big enough and humble enough to receive it. The spiritual priorities of the materially poor churches, so often rich in devotion, frequently can say something which much of the Church needs to hear. What our Lord said to people individually, applies to the whole people of God. It is easier for a camel to pass through the needle's eye than for a *retentively* rich church to lead its people into the Kingdom of Heaven.

Showing forth Christ in the many different areas of the world's need is a costly business. Only when she tries to do this, however, does the Church realize how in fact she has imprisoned Christ within institutional and self-perpetuating forms. In the inscrutable, infinite wisdom of God, that which appears to cause death so often is the seed of life.

The financial cost of the Church's involvement in the civil-rights movement in many parts of the American Church has been tremendous. Yet we read that in the Episcopal Diocese of New York, for instance, the loss occasioned by the Bishop's insistence in appointing a Negro canon of the Cathedral of St. John the Divine has been more than restored by the response of those whose faith and conscience were stimulated by his action. In California, where the Church in several places took a lead in the development of open housing opportunities, the cost has certainly been felt, but the Church's real life is none the weaker because of financial loss.

In Southern Ohio, the courageous action of the leaders of several Christian churches in publicizing firms who conform to fair employment practices has led to the falling away of some members but to the strengthening of others. In England, and in South Africa, courageous leadership in many different areas of social concern has produced rejection of the Church by many but, again, the inner life of the Church is strengthened as a result of her vitality in fulfilling her purpose.

The cost of showing Christ forth will strike most seriously at the flabbiness which envelops the Church and which the Church can most afford to lose. The cost of not showing Him is the really fearsome thing. Materially, there would be lean times ahead for the Church in many parts of the world if she were faithful to the witness for which the world is crying out. In her leanness there would be the strength of new-found virility. Maybe then there would not be quite so much to administer, not so much on which to feed our preoccupation with ourselves, but there would be more souls to care for, more time to be concerned with people in their deathly pain. The headaches caused through the administration of buildings and structures, from running committees and organizations, are nothing compared with the heartache of people searching in vain for the attention, care, and volume of effort so lavished upon the maintenance of ecclesiastical machinery.

G. K. Chesterton used to compare the Church with a beautiful stained-glass window. If seen from the outside, the Church appears to be dirty, dull, and uninteresting. Only from within does the color and light and beauty show up in all its splendor. The same might be said of the world in which Christ dwells and acts. If we look at it from the outside, we do not see it as Christ sees it, in all the glory of God's creative and redemptive love.

The Church (in M.R.I. and other movements) is trying to turn herself inside out, to look at herself and the world from the inside. To do this will hurt. Rich churches will have to share their wealth with others less fortunate, more than was ever thought possible. Poor churches will discover great riches which they too must give away. I do not believe that God separates the Church as we know it from the world as He sees it. Both are His creations and in Him, through Jesus Christ, have been made one. This is what the Incarnation tells us. It is the Church's function to proclaim this truth in a holy community which is in the world and which acknowledges Christ as King.

The Church must break through her own bonds in order to find the freedom which mutuality demands. M.R.I. must become the Anglican Church's offering to the world of our discovery of what interdependence really means. This condition, truly realized, would place the Church in the world as surely as Christ indwells the people who live in it. Then the Church could speak to a world which is realistically seen and loved. We will need to do some *listening* too—but then, deep down, dialogue is really what mutual responsibility and interdependence in the body of Christ is all about.

VI

A TIME FOR LISTENING

W<small>E</small> HAVE SEEN some of the stultifying effects upon her witness in the world of the Church's preoccupation with herself. As chaplain for six years of a large state university campus in California, I know something of the effort and expense of our concern, once we leave the established framework of the parish-oriented ministry. As one sees the development by several denominations of college work programs in the United States, there are many indications of progress. Both denominationally and, increasingly, ecumenically, a very exciting ministry to the campus is evolving.

Of all the things that the American Church can offer to the Church in other parts of the world, one of the most significant is the flexibility of much of her ministry to colleges and universities. College work is taken extremely seriously, as a glance at the budgets of the Churches would show. Presbyterians and Methodists, Episcopalians and the United Church of Christ, Roman Catholics and Lutherans, show a similar and expanding involvement with the college ministry. All this can say a great deal to us about methods of outreach elsewhere.

One of the most encouraging things about the Church's ministry to many campuses in the United States is the fact that the Christian community in the university is prepared to be a listening community. It cannot fall prey to that narrow kind of professionalism which seeks to give the impression that, within the orthodox framework of the institutional Church, there is confined the total reserve of human knowledge. Even in those academic disciplines most directly related to the Church's involvement with society, in the university of today we simply have to be better listeners than talkers. Woe betide the chaplain who attempts to swim beyond his depth. The clerical collar is not the passport to assumed knowledge, and the chaplain, like anybody else, must produce his credentials. The student cafeteria will quickly expose the phony or the overly dogmatic to exactly the same evaluation process undergone by any other stall-holder in the market place of ideas. This means, of course, that in some cases the Church becomes a private club, in retreat from a world which is seen as a threat. (Mercifully, today, few Anglican student groups on American campuses retain the name "The Canterbury Club." Nothing can be more sure of alienating the university community from what the Church does have to offer, than to have in its midst a group of pious oddballs showing the Episcopal Church at its prettiest, while the rest of the community is engaged in the adventure of ideas.)

The parish ministry can learn a great deal from the many splendid instances of the challenge presented by so-called secular society and accepted by the Church. If ever an illustration of the falsity of the distinction between the sacred and the secular is needed, the university campus surely provides it. Here God, who is truth, reveals Himself through the various academic disciplines. Here men and women, not in surplices but in white laboratory coats, and possibly some of them not even acknowledging the existence of God, are the vehicles of God's self-revelation in our discovery of the nature of the world we live in, and of the nature of our human personalities and life. It there is one place in this world which can be described as the channel through which the talent of today will be expressed in the leadership of tomorrow, the university is it. In the university, the Church can join in the search for truth, while all the time offering the challenge of a divine perspective through which truth can be seen in focus. The perspective, however, had better be something infinitely better than the pious platitude and professional gimmick all too often associated in the student mind with the Church! The Church's ministry to the campus must be superbly specialized and trained to take its place with the best that the college or university faculty can offer. Our colleges and universities offer a ready-made community, motivated, theoretically at least, by the search for knowledge. The motivation for this search varies, of course, from the pure and noble love of truth for its own sake, to the merely financial and status rewards given by the world to those who possess parts of it. Through her involvement with those motives, the Church can offer those moral values which place knowledge in the dimension of wisdom. Through her own engagement in the search for truth, the Church shares a common motivation with the campus. The foundation of the Church's offering and acceptability is her willingness to know and to share in the life of the college community.

In many parts of the world, the Church has not even begun to face up to the tremendous responsibility of ministering to the ever-growing college and university systems. In so many places we muddle along without giving any priority to the university, content to work within a parochial structure and to label it "college work." But this system no longer caters for today's division of men's interests and concerns. In all too many places, and sometimes still in the United States, the college ministry is dull, drab, unimaginative, and withered-up. Our ministry can be fertilized by the sacredness of the secular world's scramble for truth, even though its motives for the scramble are not always the highest. The university provides a drive and a challenge to the minister working in its fellowship and community. There is a stimulation to constant growth which the parochial ministry rarely offers.

For instance, one has only to see in action the Anglican program at the University of Michigan to see the relevance of a ministry clearly speaking to students where they are. It is a ministry which obviously is stimulated by the exciting challenge of the campus and is meeting it in a way which makes the Church seem to be alive. The impact of this ministry upon the university is clear for all to see. The faculty members who showed to me the alley coffee house/movie house/debating chamber and, in a real and positive sense, "church," did so with justifiable pride.

One of the problems facing the parish priest, as opposed to the college chaplain, is that of responsibility for raising money. The relative freedom of the college chaplain is provided by the fact that usually he can look to his own communion for support. In other words, we are back again to the administrative stranglehold which the need to keep the machine running has gained. So often the parish is the diocese in miniature and the parish priest, because of the structure in which he must work, has to be the jack-of-all-trades but more especially the administrator. The solution to this problem is by no means easy, but a solution must be found if the Church is to present anything to the world other than pious dress.

Isn't it true to say that in most places the image of the minister, and certainly that of the bishop, is not that of the pastor or of a man whose main communication is with God, but that of a man sitting at his desk? In the super colossal Church of our day, the seat of the average clergyman's pants gets more wear than do the knees. The bishop's desk tends to be where the decisions are made, not the altar. The parish office rather than the church has become the center of decision-making. It is not the location of the decision-making process which causes concern, but rather the apparent absence in so many cases of the altar or church as the basic point of reference to God.

We must be careful not to go overboard into that false otherworldliness which for too long has isolated the priest from people. We must retain our vision of the Church as the whole people of God, with the ordained clergyman taking his part in the community. But free ourselves from the bureaucratic stranglehold in which we are caught, we must, if the world-wide Church is to pick up the pieces and build her new life. The supernatural basis of our faith in no way is betrayed by our concern to meet people where they are. On the contrary, to do so is to be thoroughly incarnational.

In attempting to speak to "secular" society, which for long she has viewed in separation from herself, the Church has failed to be the leaven in the lump. Somehow, Christianity has become transformed into a reflection of the world's own image. The Christian community seems just like any other group within society, presenting no viable alternative to what we see around us. One consequence of this has been the removal of so many priests out of the front-line work with people, and their imprisonment behind desks—a tragic part of the price we pay for allowing the means to become the end. Of course, we need administration—and some are called indeed to be administrators in the Church—but so much of what is administered need not even exist. Today, more and more clergymen administer work involving fewer and fewer people than ever before. Is this because we are dealing with more people at greater depth, or is it that we are increasingly concerned with the perpetuation of our institution?

In all our ecumenical discussions, we Anglicans present the case for the retention of bishops. We base our argument on apostolic succession and the essential role of the bishop as shepherd. But our brethren of other Christian denominations simply do not see the bishop as the chief pastor in practice. They see him as the chief administrator, and there seems to be little apostolic precedent for that. I do not think that the Anglican Church shows in her own life the essential pastoral oversight so inbuilt in the apostolic precedents. We have made it practically impossible for the bishops to even know their clergy, let alone minister to them at any depth. Our non-Episcopal brethren are not very impressed by our concern for the preservation and exportation of episcopacy. They see, perhaps, our own need to perpetuate our status and jobs. What we need to show is that apostolic succession brings apostolic success. Seen in the mission of the Church, *this* would be convincing. To free the bishop to be the spiritual leader of his Christian community is perhaps the first step in the emancipation of the Anglican Church's ministry. The price of such freedom, we are told, would be the increase in the already top-heavy administrative structure of the Church. But this is only true if we see the Church's function in the world remaining what it now appears to be.

In a remarkable little book, published in 1914, called *The Archbishop's Test*,[1] by E. M. Green, the story is told of an Archbishop of Canterbury who decided to do away with all committees, organizations, and everything else that gave priorities to things rather than to people. It is not so much that the

---

[1]Green, E. M., *The Archbishop's Test*, Morehouse-Barlow Co., Inc., New York, re-issued 1960.

details of the story would be relevant to the situation, say, in the United States of the late nineteen sixties. What captivates the reader is the appeal to a past in which the purely pastoral role of the bishop was possible.

In the book, the archbishop

> . . . spoke of the churches as a divine society and the Prayer Book as her manual and then he touched on the truth that all the real work is done in the world through prayer, which, translated into other language, simply means that God does it, not we. Then he showed how it was the intention of the Church that daily should the Great Sacrifice be pleaded but he allowed that in some parishes that was not yet possible. Still in every parish prayers should be said daily that a perpetual intercession might go up for every estate of man. And then came in his reason for suspending the work of societies. When all was done by the Church it would be superfluous.[2]

The archbishop made it known that he was at the service of his people, and that nobody was to be precluded from seeing him if that person needed help. Needless to say, the wrath of the organization man in the Church was heaped on the archbishop's head, "dissatisfaction clamored noisily at the archbishop's door." With the Prayer Book as the basis of the Church's life, and its intentions and rubrics obeyed, a great and mighty change came over the Church throughout the land. The Church was free, and society received the benefit of her freedom and the souls of men were fed.

Maybe to change the course followed by the Church today is not as easy as the book makes out. One could guess, though, what being a member of the Christian Church would be like if people replaced buildings as the pastors' main concern. Again, it is a question of balance and of sanity, which might involve pulling oneself up for a while and stopping to stand, stare, and listen in order to learn.

---

[2]*Ibid.*, pp. 20-21.

There are people whose needs are obvious and urgent. There are the homeless, the persecuted, the lonely, the aged, the frustrated, the sick, who do not always see the Church as a community of compassion to whom they can turn. Our seminaries increasingly turn out men who are infinitely more *au fait* with parish organization and finance, than with the know-how to win souls for Jesus Christ. The souls waiting to be "won" are often a long way from the Church, at least from the Church as we know it. There are plenty of souls waiting to be fed within the structured Church, too, and often they are people most caught up in the activism of the Church's life, sitting in our pews and serving on our committees. They are victims of the glossy cover of the Church, allowed to think that being religious is doing churchy things.

If the Church does not teach God's people what the real life of Jesus Christ is really all about, then it will be too late for inspiration when the millstones around our necks pull us to our knees.

VII

THE PRIORITY OF PEOPLE

THE REVOLUTION in the Church's orientation wili have to come through a drastically sharpened perception and reassertion of basic priorities. We must sort out primary and secondary objectives. If we cannot afford in time, manpower, or money everything we would like to do, then, like any other family or community, we are going to have to be realistic and re-evaluate our position. In many cases, the priorities which are chosen must find more effective and economical ways of fulfillment. Obviously, our primary function as the Church is to effect the reconciliation between man and God, using faithfully the means which Christ has left to His Church to achieve this. We must be the laser beam of God's love, penetrating the hearts of men individually and in society, cutting cleanly and economically through apathy, ignorance, prejudice, and hostility.

A top candidate for nomination as a secondary concern of the Church's existence is administration. This, after all, is a means to an end and the end is people in their relationship with God. The amount of time, energy, and money spent on administration would make any divine audit of our material and spiritual budgets embarrassing reading. If this means doing away with much of our existing administration, so be it. The criterion for the survival of any of it must be its essential purpose in the fulfillment of the Church's ministry to people. By this criterion, the substitution of desks for people in the deployment of our ordained manpower is almost an indictable offense under the new covenant which God has made with His people through Jesus Christ. From the proliferation of "Executive Secretaries" sprouting everywhere in the Church, one would gain the impression that the Church is enjoying a boom, and that more executives are needed to handle all the business!

Such a re-evaluation of the Church's efficiency will require the bishops to measure their priorities by their own "archbishop's test." Certainly *something* drastic has to be done to redefine the function of a leader in the Church of God. (For myself, and as an Anglican reading through the consecration service, I shudder at the recurrence of the same cause for penitence in my own failure to fulfill my office as the Prayer Book intends it to be fulfilled.) Increasingly, the bishops are pulled away from their function as chief pastors and are fast becoming a combination of money raisers, committee commuters, and corporation executives. It is small wonder that a book could be written with the title *How To Become a Bishop Without Being Religious*.[1] In more cases than not, the bishop is the least accessible person in his diocese, guarded and protected from the very people whom he exists to serve. I have known it take weeks to obtain an appointment to see a bishop on a pastoral matter of urgency, and this lamentable trend is growing. Hierarchical activism is today's form of our failure to keep awake in the Church's Gethsemane in the contemporary world. It simply is not good enough for us to rationalize

---

[1] Smith, C. M., *How To Become a Bishop Without Being Religious*, Doubleday and Co., New York, 1965.

our transition from shepherd to bureaucrat by saying that we have too much to do, and therefore something must suffer. What suffers most is people, and the solution to the problem lies in where we consider our priorities to be. It really is as simple as that!

One antidote to the current trend has been found effective in the Diocese of Kimberley. Many of our priests are widely scattered in this large diocese. A year or so ago, we began to grapple seriously with the very real problem of loneliness and isolation. Through the support and eager co-operation of several organizations in the United States, such as the Episcopal Book Club in Arkansas, and The Church Periodical Club, we have been able to institute what seems to be a novel program. One book of current theological interest is supplied quarterly to all of our clergy. Meeting in four archdeaconries—or, when funds are available for transportation, all meeting centrally in the diocese—the bishop joins with his clergy in a two- or three-day study group, based upon the book which all will have read. Individual clergy are asked to prepare papers on vital questions raised by the selected book; together we seek to apply to our local conditions the main themes of the books studied. (So far, our clergy have discussed together Archbishop Ramsey's *Sacred and Secular*,[2] *The Church Today and Tomorrow* by J. V. Langmead Casserley[3] and *With Love to the Church* by Monica Furlong.[4] In addition to this, the Episcopal Book Club has supplied for all our clergy the available volumes of Francis J. Hall's *Dogmatic Theology*.[5] The entire *Church's Teaching*

---

[2]Ramsey, A. M., *Sacred and Secular,* Longmans, Green, London, and Harper & Row, New York, 1965.

[3]Casserley, J. V. Langmead, *The Church Today and Tomorrow*, S.P.C.K., London, and Morehouse-Barlow, New York, 1964.

[4]Furlong, Monica, *With Love to the Church*, Holder & Stoughton, London, 1965, and Forward Movement, Cincinnati, 1968.

[5]Hall, Francis J., *Dogmatic Theology*, republished by the American Church Union, New York, 1966.

Series[6] is to be presented to every priest in the Diocese by the Church Periodical Club.)

Many benefits result from this program. The bishop, at least four times each year, joins with his clergy in study. He is thus obliged, as are all of his priests, to establish a definite priority for private and corporate study. Over several days each quarter, he is able to bring together his clergy for sacred studies in a community and fellowship in which all participate and have something to offer. It can be seen how such a program helps remove something of the frequent isolation, spiritual and physical, so often experienced by our clergy. At the same time, it helps build up a private library for each of our priests, which otherwise would not be possible. In this way, private study—one of the most neglected areas in the life of most clergy—is encouraged and made possible.

In my own case, this program has proved more successful than could have been imagined. It is building up a very real relationship between bishop and priests which is grounded in something much more significant than merely social contact. If we bishops are too busy for this type of program, then we are just too busy. Our priorities need overhaul. I offer this program, now well launched in Kimberley, merely as one practical effort to re-evaluate this bishop's use of time. In one aspect of his work he is placed right where he belongs—with his fellow clergy—all of us searching for the Christ in that part of the vineyard committed to our care.

Sometimes, as is happening in the Church's ministry to our colleges and universities, necessary change in our ways of putting first things first will be effected by the naked revelation of needs to be met. Sometimes, more often than we think, it will require a Malcolm Boyd, praying his prayers in a vastly differ-

---

[6]The Seabury Press, New York.

ent kind of "church" than we are used to thinking of—like the "hungry i" nightclub in San Francisco. In such a case, as in fact did happen, there will be many cries of "iconoclast" from within the Church. But the very respectability of the Church as most people see her needs such iconoclasm if the barriers to effective communication are to be broken down.

Where the majority of people are to be found, the Church is rarely to be seen. Industry, universities, and, yes, night life too, are clamoring for attention in the vast sociological complexities of our century. We live in a very complex world in which the Church is structured to meet people only partially where they live their lives. This is because our real involvement with our people stops when they leave the doors of their homes to go into the world. It is a world in which the institutional Church is scarcely to be found, but in which the Church is very much represented by her members.

We have become riveted, unconsciously so, perhaps, in our assumption that people are where we would like to think they are—in suburbia, falling within a neat parish system. In allowing ourselves to drift into an almost total concern with suburbia we flounder in bewilderment at the problems of downtown. Because so little is known about the spiritual no man's land where our people live out most of their daily lives, we tend to be powerless and ineffective when they bring problems home with them which cannot be contained in the average parish program.

The idea that God is dead certainly has aroused plenty of public interest. If the Church were manifesting a truly living God, desperately concerned with politics, economics, family life, public and private morality, civil rights, in short with every area of man's life, then the idea that God is dead would be manifestly absurd. He would be seen and known to be very much alive!

The fact that so many people have been unable to find God anywhere in society, and often least of all in the Church, is a shattering indictment of the Church's lack of involvement with everyday life. If in Church people can find only a reflection of themselves in their Sunday suits, then it is a salutary thing that the people have not confused themselves with God. It is also salutary that the vast majority of people, whatever they think they are searching for, be it called self-identity or fulfillment, reject peripheral discoveries as being the totality of God.

The point is that the whole "God is dead" debate is itself a manifestation of searching for God who, through His Church, should be constantly seen and known. It is a laudable refusal on the part of thinking people, who cannot be dismissed as "cranks," to accept a theoretical God. There is no life in a static theology which fails to tie up the search for truth with a Christ who indwells every part of the world. If God appears to be dead, then the Church has conducted the burial service. If this seems harshly judgmental, it is written in tremendous sympathy with the search for God which would not be so painful if the Church were doing her job.

The almost total rejection by the vast mass of society in most countries of the world of the institutionalized Church, has led to a desperate search for a God who is sought in bottle and drug, sex and topless show *à la* go-go. To really put a kick into religion, the world can offer L.S.D. and a trip into almost instant mystical experience. Capsule religion in its many different forms shows the dissatisfaction with what the world can offer, as well as that which the Church has offered. People are as "religious" as ever they were, because it is their nature to be. To the "unchurched" millions, however, Christianity is just another drab formula—drab because they can only know of it what they see in us—and they are not impressed. This is why the Church surely must break out from her pulpits and stained glass, her buildings and her committees and go where the people are. Again, it is the sense of proportion and balance I yearn to see, and I think my conscious yearning is shared subconsciously by many who are on the "outside" of the Church.

When people hear the word of God in the nightclubs of this world, then maybe the Church, like the sleeping beauty, will realize that she is awakening from her long sleep. When she does this, Christ will be waiting for us in the strangest places. Maybe He will not often be seen in cassock, surplice, and other ecclesiastical trappings. Certainly He will not necessarily be either an American Episcopalian or a white South African Calvinist!

Our re-evaluation of priorities must put on the zoom lens for a close-up view, both of our existing parish structures and of our much more recent incursions into the weekday arena of life where the people of God work.

The almost exclusive concentration upon the parish as the main unit of the Church's outreach increasingly appears to be misplaced. Industrial mission, the worker priest movement, the college campus, the inner city mission, the itinerant group and team ministries—all these are the commando units of the Church militant today. The parish system is geared to a pattern of life which, in the great industrial societies of the world, shows the most violent change in the social revolution of our time. Men and women are out of their homes more than they are in them. Increasingly today, husbands and wives work, either from choice or necessity. The focal point of life is much more likely to be the place where a living is made than where the family life is lived. Of course, this is tragic. What we must realize, however, is that the parish cannot encompass anything more than a part of the whole life of our people, and that therefore there is serious imbalance in our almost exclusively parish-centered structure. The parish is able to function most effectively when it can concentrate upon that part of life which it is geared to serve, namely, man's life in home and family. This used to be the hub of the wheel of his entire life. Except in rural areas and undeveloped countries, it is no longer the case. The home as the stable center of achievement has been usurped by the place of work which has become the comparatively unstable center of ambition.

The grouping of people has become enlarged from the old family pattern. Business and professional groups, social and labor unions, schools and personal interest groups—here is where people now live and move and search for themselves and the meaning to their lives. Whether we like it or not, the parochial structure of the Church is primarily directed to the leisure time of man. Of man's leisure, the Church lays claim to a share. Though leisure may be increasing in the affluent societies, so that man now has more time free of work than ever before, this is not where his life is shaped and fashioned.

The layman's obedience is to the world: this is why so few can honestly give it to a Church which is not seen to be a part of his everyday world. His primary obedience is not even given to the private retreat he calls his home, so dependent for its existence upon the world. It is to this world where our new forms of ministry must be directed. It is this world where man must give his time and talents and which is the source of his deepest fears, frustrations, hopes, and gratifications.

It is futile to try to clericalize the layman and pretend that, by performing his churchly duties on Sundays, his Christian life is given all the expression necessary for its fulfillment. The concept of the Church as a domestic congregation revolving around the clergyman, who is the motivator, the administrator, the approver of the congregation's corporate activity, is crippling our capacity to evolve outward to meet the needs of modern society. It allows us to pour our energies, resources of time, talent, and money into only a partial relationship with people and their needs. What is given on Sunday to the people of God is not easily carried over to Monday and the rest of a week during which the Church is neither seen nor heard.

We have become so cemented in our parish structure that often we hear that the only work for which a new priest or minister can be considered is a parish. "Go to a good parish, my boy—that is where you will learn the ground rules of your ministry." In all probability, that is precisely where he will learn to perpetuate the system. He will see the Church in its Sunday best, and, if he is not very careful, will ignore a throbbing world which ceases to throb on Sunday when we like to think that the Church takes over. Church to most people is for when the world shuts down. But Christ is in the factories, laboratories, classroom, and shops on Monday morning as surely as He was in Church on Sunday. I am convinced that in his heart of hearts the layman feels the contrast between what we offer and what he needs. He could help provide a great deal for himself within his own proper ministry. To do this, he must first be taught what his ministry is and released from the restrictions which, in the past, have been placed upon him.

It was a sobering thought which Sam Wylie[7] gave to a group of us who were attending a chaplains' conference some years ago in San Francisco. "The Church uses methods to attract the men of the twentieth century which, in the nineteenth century, she used to attract women." There was laughter at the time, but the truth of what was said made our laughter hollow.

---

[7]Then, of the Episcopal Church's National Division of College Work; now Dean of the General Theological Seminary, New York.

VIII

BEYOND PAROCHIALISM

Is ALL THAT has gone before an insidious attempt to suggest that there is no further use for the parochial framework of the Church's ministry? Not at all—it is rather an assertion of misplaced priorities in the deployment of the dwindling reserves of the Church's manpower.

Of course the Church must continue to provide Christ's ministry to men, women, and children as individuals and as families where they live. The Church has a great deal to say to a world in which family life is a victim of man's misplaced, though understandable, allegiances. One of the most recognized roles of the Church is to speak to man in his family environment. To help avert the further fragmentation of the family unit into stratified wider community groupings is to meet one of the critical needs of our century, psychologically and sociologically. The problem of maintaining the family unit as the generator of a larger response to life in a wider social community bewilders our society. The demands of family and society so often seem to be in conflict. The tragic consequences of such confusion are seen in divorce and juvenile courts.

Once again, even in the area of life in which she is most firmly entrenched, the Church has not exerted decisive influence in shaping man's capacity to meet the conflict of living in a changing world. This is because again we stand on the outside, looking in. Structure and inflexibility, professionalism and all its barriers, prevent the layman from seeing the Church as desperately concerned with *his* problems. Our alternative to what the world offers as its own solutions is a very valid one; all sound theology must be sound psychology too. The dislocation of family life is in conflict both with good theology and also with the deepest experience of man's needs. That we understand this must be shown from our experience for the inside of where the pain and the joy is, if our family priorities are to be communicated.

Theologically, sociologically, and psychologically, the family is the unit of corporate relationship. In it, men, women, and their children will find their individual expression of love and intimate fellowship necessary for the fulfillment of life as we are born to live it. In short, "The family is rooted in the elemental processes of life itself."[1] It is precisely because men and women who are husbands and wives, fathers and mothers, spend much more time away from their homes than in them, that the hours which are spent together as a family are critical in the stabilization and growth of elemental individual and community values. Building a home out of a house is a function of the family community. A house can be bought. It can be luxuriously furnished as an achieved goal of labor's rewards. To the world, it can look all that a house should be, the fulfillment of what downtown can offer. Any house may boast swimming pool, color TV, right neighborhood and status. But none of these make a house into a home. A home is a house with love in it, where Christians can care for each other

---

[1] *The Lambeth Conference Report*, S.P.C.K., London, and The Seabury Press, New York, 1958, "Report on the Family in Contemporary Society," 2.142.

through mutually recognized values which each sets upon the other. It is where there can be freedom to love, to fulfill the purpose of existence by exercising freedom to be truly ourselves. Home is where individuals are not separated either by fear or by rejection, but in the community of a family which has reproduced love in its existence and growth.

The Christian family has been defined as follows:

> Unlike many families in the world it will not be turned in on itself, keeping itself to itself and so losing touch also with God. In so far as it is open and exposed to the Spirit of God, it will share in the ministry of the Church to society, caring for friend and neighbor, near or distant, not seeking privileges for itself, a forgiving society where free and fresh starts are always possible, a beacon light to a factious, unforgiving, and suspicious world.[2]

The priority of the family in the Church's ministry was well recognized by the 1958 Lambeth Conference of bishops of the Anglican Communion:

> The Church has to be vigilant on its behalf, receptive of the influences on society, friendly to good home making, critical of the pressures which may become hurtful, remembering that, in the past, Christians and philanthropists have been far too ready to deplore, and far too content to do no more than ambulance work. Our duty is to be, as far as we can, at the creative end of social processes, as the Church unfortunately failed to be in the early days of the industrial revolution in the West.

"To be . . . at the creative end of social processes" is the key to our fulfillment in Christ's total ministry, and the family of today is certainly caught up in one of the most grueling so-

---

[2]*Ibid.*, 2.153.

cial processes of our time. The Church must be a part of all the many strands of life which today envelop the family, the home, and all that they mean. To do this we will have to realize the complexities of modern life. We must learn to develop our involvement not only with the family internally on Sundays, but also with the fragmented family unit on Mondays, following each member in school, office, and market place. What seems to be necessary is not the abolition of the family caring unit called the parish. Rather is it our awareness that total concentration upon man in his family setting will fall far short of direct involvement in his total life.

The imbalance in our established methods of training priests, almost exclusively for the parish ministry, is yet another cause of anxiety. Also, it is our poor deployment of the clergy who are trained that bothers me. Whether this deployment be at the opposite ends of the spectrum of priorities—behind administrators' desks or exclusively in parishes, the Christian Church should be very concerned about the consequences. Our concept of mission—Christ's outreach to our Father's world—is defensive. Mission on the defense can hardly hope to succeed in the divine offensive of love, to speak, and to be the good news to the world.

Man in his family must be seen in the perspective of man in his total society. He must be cared for realistically and compassionately in a much more flexible home-based Christian community than our professionally oriented structure of parish can at present allow. He must also be cared for from Monday through Saturday, when he lives his life in a world which constantly challenges, threatens, and, more often than professional clergy think, crucifies him when he is alone. These are the times when Christ's "professional" disciples, to many people, seem to be so unconcerned that they might just as well be sleeping.

Kimberley, South Africa, is indeed a long way from the United States or Britain. The problems with which we are grappling, in the right use of overstretched clergy and inadequate resources to meet our bulging needs, are very much the same the world over, however. In the city of Kimberley, with a population of around 75,000 people, we have six Anglican parishes, including the Cathedral. Recently, we have created out of our non-Cathedral parishes a group ministry. It is hoped that this team will develop along the specialist vocations of the priests engaged in it. Old parochial jurisdictions, drawn up along purely arbitrary boundaries, will wither. From the professional clergy trap of established geographical authority will evolve, it is hoped, jurisdiction by vocation. Vocation, we anticipate, will replace geography as the criterion of concern. It makes so much sense to use clergy in this way. The individual minister could not possibly cope with the volume and specialized variety of work which he was called upon to do. With a shortage of clergy paralyzing the Church's mission, the constant overlapping and duplication of work are negative factors no business organization could afford to tolerate. Yet, in city after city throughout the world, we find parishes working independently of each other and proud of it: each one jealously preserving its own jurisdiction and patron saint: each one subjecting its parishioners to a whirligig of liturgical, doctrinal, and organizational change: each one depending upon the whims and abilities of its revolving clergymen.

The success of our Kimberley experiment has yet to be proved, but there is no doubt that the spirit and community life of the members of our group ministry have changed for the better. We have added to the group lay workers, working within their own vocational speciality—not as side kicks or assistants to the clergy "leaders," but as equal participating members of the group—a welfare nurse, a secretary, a Christian stewardship specialist, and a Sunday School adviser. Out of an old, struggling set of independent churches, each going its own way, we are evolving a Christian community of the whole people of God, acknowledging their interdependence in a relationship which shows its validity by a reinvigorated life.

When I went to Oxford to study law, before I would lay claim to being anything but an observer of the Church, the number of churches and their proximity to one another amazed me. When I served as a curate in one of them, the tolerated redundancy of many became even more a source of wonder. To a lesser degree perhaps, but still glaringly anomalous in a Church which has a struggle to maintain itself, many dioceses in Britain and the United States illustrate the same problem.

The Church's ministry to the family is a vital part of our total ministry to men and women where they are. It is, however, only a part, but, where we provide it, considerable and urgent changes in our structures are necessary if this is not to become strangled by our traditional forms.

From our own experimental group ministry in Kimberley, there is developing an itinerant ministry to outlying areas. Previously, conforming with the English tradition, church buildings were put up in every village. Today, churches which simply cannot justify their continued independent existence are being brought within the group. Obviously, a group or team ministry, working together in specialized and vocational programs, is very much more flexible than the old, relatively immovable, parochial form. Now, by centralizing the group, the Church can meet some of the many problems caused by the loneliness of our clergy living in isolated areas. By sending out men in apostolic fashion to minister to our outlying districts, where there are scattered families and small congregations, our people are cared for in the family context. This means, in its turn, that precious capital frozen in churches attended only monthly or weekly at best can be freed for more urgent use. The cost of mobilizing our priests and providing, as is our intention, caravan churches, is more than covered by absence of maintenance and capital recovery on redundant, therefore disposable, church buildings. Such a program of changed structure has been applied in other parts of the Anglican Communion with varying degrees of success, but our Kimberley experiment certainly could help evolve new patterns of outreach. These may encourage other areas with similar problems to break with traditional forms which perpetuate rather than solve those problems. The priority of meeting people's needs demands changing frontiers in the Church's ministry. Our mission to man in his family and home is no exception to that imperative. In the re-evaluation of our priorities, and of our capacity to meet them, purely sentimental retention of either buildings or structures is a luxury we cannot afford.

When we turn our attention to man in his workday environment, we do not have anything equivalent to the parish structure on which to build a more relevant ministry. It is here that we have failed so miserably; it is at the weekday level where we have the most challenging opportunities to experiment and to evolve new patterns of outreach. Once we can release the conservative brake of enormous investment in buildings, methods, and fossilized structures, we can begin to move forward. It is in ministering to man in his city, which is also the city of God, that we have our greatest freedom of action.

Should our action be based simply on an extension of what we have already in the parishes? It would be difficult to apply most existing Church programs, even in downtown parishes, to factory, shop, office, or consulting room. Totally different techniques must be evolved. The place of work cannot be seen as merely an extension of home minus family. One thing is sure, the professional clergyman, ministering to life in its urban setting, will not remain the hub around which the whole wheel revolves, as he has become in most of our parishes. His ministry and that of the layman will merge into a single apostolate.

Whatever we do to meet the needs of man in our sprawling cities must not be a nostalgic, backward look for inspiration to rural England. Neither can it be the perpetuation of St. Augustine's "fantastic distinction," as Reinhold Niebuhr has described it, between the "Two Cities," which has developed into the fatal separation of the Church and the world. This separation has dogged the Church's ministry for hundreds of years, until now we are hoist on our own petard. The Church is not in competition with the world; we are a part of it. "We must be able to see the hand of God in the technical and social revolution, sharing in it, not simply deploring it or preaching at it 'from over the hedges'."[3] Christian social witness must precede direct evangelism. To do this the Christian must seek to interpret what God is saying through the existential situation in industry and society.

A good deal of biblical reinterpretation will be necessary, too, before we can structure a twentieth century servant ministry to our hierarchically power-structured society. The social gospel undoubtedly applies to impersonal power situations as it does to persons individually. There will be development and evolution in all areas when we learn to act with Christ in the world today. Such a projection calls for spiritual perception of a high order. Our perception will come only with our identification and direct sharing in real life situations where God is at work outside the Church's recognizable ministry. Again we must become a listening Church before we can speak and act really decisively.

---

[3]Phipps, Simon, *God On Monday*, Holder & Stoughton, London, 1966.

Bishop Paul Moore, in his book, *The Church Reclaims the City*,[4] has provided a jumping-off point for urban action. In a chapter headed "Notes on a Theology of Urban Work," he discusses the wide range of Christian theology in the light of contemporary metropolitan life. Without such a theological map, the Church will merely extend existing institutionalism and inward preoccupation to her work in the city.

> In every city there is a group of men who are shaping the future of that city. Often they are unconscious of their role; always they are being shaped by impersonal economic and sociological forces beyond their control. Nevertheless, they make decisions in a forum of ideas: in the board rooms of industry, in the city council, in the ongoing tension between the idealism of the city planner and the pragmatism of the Chamber of Commerce. Here is a lay ministry: to discover the theological principles involved and to apply to the shape of things to come such principles as diversity in unity (the Trinity) and personhood within community (the Communion of Saints). Such a ministry can be backed by the power of a Church which has its representatives in every related institution and which has come to realize that the modern metropolis need not be a Babylon. Let the Church, then, sense her role in the creation of the city in which she dwells![5]

We are seeing, in several countries, a growth in the number of industrial chaplains, and this is good. We have already mentioned the advance guard of the Church's involvement at some depth with the "secular," in our campus ministries.

Already in the United States, Britain, and now in South Africa, group and team ministries are probing beyond existing structures of parish ministry for new forms, and penetrating

---

[4]Moore, Paul, *The Church Reclaims the City*, The Seabury Press, New York, 1964.
[5]*Ibid.*, pp. 46-47.

involvement in society. In many urban churches there is a new look to Christian outreach; pilot programs designed to establish realistic inner city ministries in the United States are under way. Churches of different denominations are finding, in the urban ministry, fruitful expressions of ecumenical activity. The needs are so great and manifest that no one denomination can even begin to meet them. Manpower and money considerations preclude the duplication of facilities. The inadequacy of existing provisions provide no incentive to hang on to what we already have. Nowhere can ecumenical Christian ministry find more urgent and obvious application than the city. After all, it is occupied by men and women already united in their aim to earn a living.

All of this is exciting and shows that the Church is really searching to meet the Christ indwelling His people where they are. Book after book is being published showing concern for greater meaning in mission. It is thrilling to live in a time of revolution in the Church, not only theological but also social. The social revolution which the world has undergone at first seemed to have passed the Church by. It looked as though the Church had retreated into her castle hoping that she would escape the tumult of change. Today, the Church is moving into territory long neglected. It is like stepping into the dark—but for the people of God there is good precedent for such a journey. In our gradual emancipation from the exclusiveness of the parish system, we have a tough road ahead, and there are few signposts to show us the way. Where the Church must head for is really not very far. Where people are is where the Church is called to be.

The enemy is not the world. We fight the forces of evil manifesting themselves in our pride, selfishness, faithlessness, and fears. There will be little long-range theological artillery called for; the Church has relied too long on this. There will be a good deal of close-in combat, for which at the moment we are not as well prepared as we should be.

The answer, of course, lies in the emancipation of the lay apostolate. In opening up the great untapped reserves of talent, vocation, and spiritual power of our laity which have been allowed to lie dormant for so long, we have the key to the Church's future service. In the Church of the new order, the role of the professional clergyman will have to undergo considerable redefinition. At long last, in our awakening to the Church's place in the world, we might be able to free both clergy and laity to see their respective and joint vocations in the world.

That there is a passionate yearning on the part of many to consecrate their talents, and to "do something" for the world, is seen in the birth and development of the Peace Corps. Service groups and societies abound throughout the world. Governmental agencies have tried to educate and channel selfless motives in forms which give to the individual opportunities for creative expression of usefulness. Secular society in fact has taken a dynamic lead in recognizing such expression as a positive need in the lives of men. The Church vacation programs for students and the Church World Service have only limited appeal. When the Church can be seen as a world-wide peace corps herself, with all Christians as members, there will be unending opportunities for Christian action. Such action will be limited only by the extent of our ability to perceive need. There are no denominational boundaries around human needs. No longer do we see our fellow Christians as the only people whom we must help. To be met, it is not necessary that human need first be baptized.

The journey of faith which we are called to take will find

the people of God marching, more often stumbling, toward the city. Our task is to prevent the city of men from becoming a spiritual desert. It is, in fact, to reunite the two great cities so long kept apart—the city of men and the City of God.

IX

WHERE THE ACTION IS—THE APOSTOLATE OF THE LAITY

IF ₁THE CHURCH has a hope of being "at the creative end" of the social process, then to gain freedom for the laity to exercise their ministry is an urgent necessity. If the stratified distinction between the two cities is to be seriously challenged by the Church, the laity must rebel against their long accepted status as doorkeepers in the house of God. For good reason, the layman has been called "the Church's secret weapon."[1] For far too long, concern with the Church's domestic housekeeping has kept dormant and untapped the vast resources of talent, energy, and vocation which lay Christians possess.

Just as the structures of the Church drastically need to be overhauled in order to be flexible enough to meet the challenge of the social revolutions that are sweeping the world, so our concept of the lay ministry demands urgent redefinition. Awareness of this necessity is shown by the many recent books dealing with it. Considerable attention is now being given to the development of exciting and challenging lay programs, particularly in the United States and Great Britain.

---

[1]Morehouse, Clifford P., *A Layman Looks at the Church*, The Seabury Press, Inc., New York, 1964, p. 167.

103

Concern to redefine the layman's role in the life of the Church is by no means limited to the Anglican Church. The ecumenical potential in expressing our concern for the lay ministry is obvious. Because of the long neglect of the layman's ministry throughout the Christian Church, the controversial questions which the ordained ministry raises in ecumenical conversation usually need not arise. Roman Catholic and many Protestant Churches alike are taking monumental steps to release the layman from the subordinate and atrophied position that he has occupied in the life of the Christian community. There are hopeful signs that many of the steps can be taken by the Churches together.

Particularly in the hierarchical churches revolving around the professional minister, the usual role of the lay man and woman is all too familiar. There is a game which most people have played at some time or another. The layman provides the collection, which he then takes up to the clergyman. He serves on the usual committees but the professional is almost automatically chairman ex officio. The layman is seen merely as the unpaid lackey of the professional clergyman; he is the goose that lays the egg which we hope may be golden.

If the situation is changing now, it is none too soon. If there is an urgent need for a crash educational program on the meaning of Christian stewardship, the same is surely true of the place of the layman in the Church. In fact, the two educational programs might well be combined in terms of the Church's own stewardship of her lay resources and the layman's stewardship of his time and talents. But before we embark on a hit or miss program of unco-ordinated lay activity, we must be perfectly clear as to the theological foundation on which we hope to act, for only then can we act out of real conviction.

The essential role of the professional clergy is to teach and to inspire, and so the first official stage of the struggle should be directed at the clergy themselves. The unofficial movement can begin now, however, for there are plenty of shots for the layman to fire!

The layman is a minister of the Church with a special vocation. He has a built-in entree into some parts of society from which the clergyman, with rare exceptions, is excluded at anything deeper than a periphery social level. The theological basis of any teaching program on the role of the laity is a simple one. The laity are the people of God and they, together with the ordained clergy, make up the Church militant on earth. To use a New Testament expression, together we are "the brethren" (I Cor. 6:1).

The distinction between the ordained and the lay ministry is essentially functional and not qualitative. There is simply no biblical ground for any value distinction of the lay and professional ministry in terms of temporal vocation. It would be completely unscriptural to define the priest in terms of "the spiritual" and the layman in terms of "the secular" and then to place relative values on the vocation of each.

In recent years, the thinking of the Roman Catholic Church has placed the laity in a very new light. One of the most challenging books to come out of the new look movement has been written by Yves Congar, O.P., *Lay People in the Church,*[2] a study for a theology of laity.

> The starting point now [Fr. Congar writes] is the idea of the People of God, the whole of it active, the whole of it consecrated, the whole a witness and sign of the purpose of God's grace for the imparting of that purpose to the world. The

[2]Congar, Yves, *Lay People in the Church*, Geoffrey Chapman, Ltd., London, and Newman Press, Westminster, Maryland, 1964.

whole living People as a structure; the dynamic sign of salvation which it represents and plants in the world as a structure:
thus the hierarchical fact is set within this whole People of
God, living and sent but without dividing its mission into
specialised parts. There are particular forms of exercise of
the Church's mission, but there is no particular mission dif-
ferentiating the faithful and the ministerial priesthood. . . .
the lay faithful in their own way carry on the Church's evan-
gelising mission, the communication of the good news of
salvation.[3]

In any practical examination of the lay apostolate in action,
the need to produce in practice what is demanded by the
Church's mission is clear and urgent. From this standpoint,
our redefinition no longer involves us in searching for "Church
work" for the laity. The opportunity is sought for the whole
people of God to exercise Christ's own ministry in fellowship
with one another in Jesus Christ. Just as when Christ commissioned the seventy to work side by side with the apostles,
so today we must recruit the total Christian ministry to infil-
trate and open up to Christ every level of our human social
structures. In this objective, the laity has a role which our
ecclesiastical structures have made almost impossible to be
fulfilled. The professional clergy cannot compete with the layman's accepted position within what we often see as the rival
city. The lay man and woman are the irreplaceable vehicles of
Christ's ministry in the actual circumstances and events of daily
life. They must be set free to restore the balance to a ministry
so long defective by the practical absence of the laity's contribution to it. Christ will use His disciples wherever their own
lives intercept the world.

If we are to evaluate our priorities accurately, the first step
must be the release of the layman from many of the tasks

---

[3]*Ibid.*, p. 25.

assigned to him. If the almost exclusively parochial structured center of his ministry is to be replaced with his own vocationally centered service, something has to give. For instance:

> It may be that an occasional scholar must give up a junior department Sunday school class, membership on a board of trustees or in a men's brotherhood group, in order to take on the responsibilities of a Christian intellectual. It will be important for clergy and fellow churchmen to realize that he is not giving up his Church work in order to do so![4]

In other words, what is called for is a massive and immediate shift in our basic attitudes as to what "Church work" really is.

This is not to say that the housekeeping chores usually assigned to the laity are unimportant. They are secondary duties which have absorbed so much time and attention that all the capacity for dynamic outreach has withered up. Of course, somebody is needed to take up the collection. Of course, Sunday morning ushering will remain a courtesy of the Church to her members. And, of course, much of the parish housework will be done rightly by lay people; but all these things will be seen in their perspective. We are speaking of sensitivity to the needs for redeployment of the unordained as well as ordained ministers of the Church.

A right use of manpower will depend upon a heightened perception of the role which the whole Church is called to play as a human agent of Christ's ministry. Perhaps even more than the ordained clergy, the laity of the institutional Church have been sucked inward by the vacuum of the Church's retreat from the world. It is this state of affairs which must be changed. It is inconceivable that the huge variety of talent contained within any parish congregation should be used solely

---

[4]Wylie, Samuel J., *New Patterns for Christian Action*, The Seabury Press, Inc., New York, 1959, p. 64.

within the professionally centered structure. It must be redirected outward in a servant ministry not to ourselves but to the world.

At the beginning, in order to free the apostles for more urgent tasks in the fast-growing Church, it was the deacon's job to serve at tables. Now the practical diaconate seems to have been assumed by the women of the Church. The deacons may have become freed to serve their apprenticeship for an automatically assumed priesthood, but the women have been taken up a one-way street leading to the parish kitchen, altar guild, and choir. This may be all nice and proper, but opportunities for service so often seem to stop there. In many dioceses our women cannot even be delegates at Convention! Surely it is time to remove the stop signs freeing our women to exercise their unique ministry, teaching and encouraging them in their apostolate of caring outreach to family and society?

If the Church, as a result, becomes less of an extension of the tennis club or "women's social fellowship," so much the better. Christianity may then have something more poignant to offer to the world than the luncheon with a "meditation" squeezed in between the *hors d'oeuvre* and the entree.

When we look at the ministry offered to women through parishes outside the United States and Canada, its very drabness and lack of imagination beggars description. An attempt to reorganize along American organizational lines, made by the women of the Church in South Africa, is not even off the ground. It is heavy going because so little has been *expected* of women's vocations in the Church. Organizations are no good unless the purpose is clear, expressed without the usual pious cliches which turn off any woman with a spark of initiative in her.

One thing must be said for churchwomen in England and

South Africa—by and large, they are emancipated from their American sisters' extraordinary preoccupation with wearing hats in church! One of the saner results of World War II was the dispensation by necessity from the need to cover up the female glory. In the United States this has yet to come. Occasionally Kleenex tissues and little lace numbers are still handed out by ladies whose task as mistresses of the wardrobe apparently is to see that no uncovered female head at worship offends the God who created it. I believe that the reason for St. Paul's concern that heads were not uncovered in church was that an uncovered head suggested a lady of ill repute and dubious profession. So if the cap fits, ladies, maybe it should be worn. Even so, let us be clear about our priorities in church!

If the true place of the layman in the Church is to be realized, the professional clergy will need to prepare the laity for their encounter with a world which may well resent their intruded witness. A developed program will require an imaginative teaching ministry based on highly specialized training. Well-thought-out guide lines leading out of the parish church must be evolved. A sharpened awareness will be necessary of the conditions in which the lay apostolate is required to function.

Already, there have been admirable attempts in the United States to assist the clergy to perform this function. Training courses are available with a strong "secular" orientation. In such courses, the clerical collar comes off and the often sheltered clergyman has to go out in the big wide world without the protection of his uniform, find a job, and pay his own way. Even though he knows that he has the security of his professional ministry to return to, it must be a salutary experience for a priest to share and experience some of the fears, the hardships, and the temptations that come with the scramble to earn a living.

Chicago, for instance, since 1963 has had its Urban Training Center which offers an opportunity for both clergy and laity to learn to live and work in all strata of urban life. In New Haven, too, a similar program more recently has been developed; groups of clergy "take the plunge" and are immersed in the daily life of urban poverty. They feel personally the experience of isolation and rejection which is the daily fate of many people to whom they are called to minister. They experience what it is like to ask for handouts, to spend a night outdoors or in a shelter for homeless men. A meal and a flop as the reward for attending a religious service initiate participants in the programs to the only view of religion that many underprivileged people receive.

In losing their visible identity as priests, participants in the urban training courses learn to find it again by sharing pain. Such programs can only begin to touch the surface of the misery and degradation of the urban poor, but at least they are a welcome beginning. Now they must be developed and encouraged for both clergy and laity, as the trail blazers they are to a more meaningful and relevant ministry.

It was once my privilege, in San Diego, California, to take part in a remarkable laymen's program developed by a parish priest.[5] For two years, a hand-picked team of laymen, representing most walks of life, met not only for several nights a week but for several weekends each year. A theological basis for their apostolate was laid by a retired priest specifically responsible for a program of theological education which many a priest could have attended with profit. The men learned to live together and in group sessions to explore their own anxieties, doubts, and vocations to this particular ministry. Only after completing an intensive course were they designated "lay min-

---

[5]Harold B. Robinson, now Episcopal Bishop of Western New York.

isters." They then took their share in parish visiting, the ministry to the sick, leadership of Bible study programs, intercession groups, and many other co-ordinated programs of outreach within their own specialized fields. Thus a Christian attorney was specifically charged to enliven the concept of justice among his brother lawyers, a Christian doctor had an apostolate to his fellow practitioners. Businessmen, teachers, aircraft factory workers, all had specific missions for which they were trained.

It is one thing for a lawyer to speak to his colleagues in terms of the Christian concept of human dignity and freedom, and another thing for a priest to attempt to do this. A Christian doctor can witness far more effectively to his colleagues than can a clergyman to the possession by man of a soul as well as a body. Care for the whole life of man in which physical healing is one part of Christ's ministry can be shared by doctor and priest in mutually accepted partnership. To the Christian teacher the enormous responsibility of communicating what wisdom really means must become reflected in the quality and integrity of his concern for the young minds who will receive such a ministry.

The clergyman cuts little ice with the businessman or the trade unionist, each of whom finds it very difficult indeed to translate the average Sunday morning sermon into ethical practices which may cost money on Monday. The fact that the laborer is worthy of his hire, provides a sound scriptural foundation for the efforts of labor unions. It also provides a solemn responsibility and charge on the Christian businessman. The factory worker needs in his midst a disciple of Jesus Christ who is not content with the shoddy and the easy way to make a dollar, but who is seeking honestly to do all things to the glory of God. This will be shown in the quality of what he produces; to him it will be his form of service to his fellow men. As a result of this attitude, the factory worker is going to learn more about integrity and fulfillment than by anything the clergyman is likely to say.

The laymen's training program of that San Diego church was more successful than anything which I had previously seen. It required tremendous preparation by the clergy and a complete reorientation of parish priorities. The life injected into a large downtown parish, however, suggested that religion was finding its way out of the Church and into the surrounding world.

Any training program for the joint ministry of laity and clergy completely rejects the passive position which most laymen are required to adopt. The consumers become producers. The idea of merely receiving spiritual handouts from the professional clergy dies a natural death when the layman is allowed to make his own contribution. In such programs, the ordained and the unordained members of the Church begin to understand what it means to be "fellow citizens with the saints and all the household of God" (Eph. 2:19). Sunday worship in the parish becomes invigorated by what the lay team can offer God together with their clergy. Intercessions become relevant to the world in which the congregation lives; thanksgiving becomes living prayer; confession and petition become related to events and needs; and adoration somehow flows from the world into the Church which has become a part of it again. The parish becomes a team in the local community—a sharing, outreaching servant team of Christians who communicate joy in their total ministry. But such experiences of what a parish in action can be like are rarely found. Because of church structures, the lead usually must come from the clergyman, who, generally speaking, is not equipped either by training or inclination to encourage such a threatening assault on his own established position.

In most cases, the necessary revolution in his own parish must be initiated by the layman. He must become the burr under the clergy saddle. He must be encouraged to enter into dialogue with the clergy—and dialogue essentially is a two-way communication. The professionals must become more responsive to the right of the laity to take their proper place in the whole ministry of Christ. The fact that the right is not often demanded should be a cause of deep concern rather than one of complacency.

In many parishes, for instance, it is the custom to provide opportunities following the preaching of the sermon for the congregation to "come back" with disagreements, questions, and their own contributions. In almost every case, this has a salutary effect on the quality of preaching, which usually needs all the help it can get. The over-all standard of preaching by professional and supposedly trained clergymen is appalling. It is one thing for the clergyman to soliloquize from the pulpit but quite another for him to be subjected to the critical examination of what he has said by those who have heard him.

If one of the functions of the professional minister is to prepare the layman for his ministry in the world, his teaching ministry must go far beyond the pious platitudes of the sermons which inspire only the funny story. How many people who saw the show, or have heard the record, *Beyond the Fringe,* recognized in mannerism, accent, and content the exaggerated realism of which good satirical comedy is made? The sermon "preached" in that show on the text "Esau my brother is a hairy man, but I am a smooth man" (Gen. 27:11), was brilliantly successful because its shattering irrelevance had an authenticity which must have struck the chords of memory in audience after audience which found it hilariously funny. If our secret weapon is to be launched, the launching pad had better not be a joke!

X

A BLUEPRINT FOR REVOLT

WHAT ARE THE vulnerable points that can be pinpointed by the laity in their revolt against the structured Church which has imprisoned their vocation for so long? An obvious candidate for attack is the clerical professionalism which expresses "priestcraft" in its worst forms. The presence of so much of this is not always the clergyman's fault. Often he is a victim of the structure in which he is trained to work.

Whether he likes it or not, in many cases from the moment he enters a seminary the clergyman is prepared for initiation into the Church's equivalent of a closed college fraternity. Particularly within the English tradition at least, he is taught to conform to a pattern of behavior which is expected of the parson. Often, extremes of behavior are produced. One recognizable form is in the ghastly heartiness of the back-slapping priest who says "damn" in order to be one of the chaps. Another manifestation is in the pious timidity of the gorgeously arrayed, sanctuary prima donna, who would rather die than expose his insecurities by wearing jeans and a sweat shirt during a weekend of fellowship with his leading laymen. This, of course, is exaggerated and a big generalization, but will be recognized as being not entirely devoid of truth. The Church, like any other institution, has its "characters."

The vast majority of clergymen are men who have honestly tried to devote their lives to the service of God at considerable cost to themselves and to their families. But, equally, the vast majority of clergymen tend to be bewildered by the dichotomy between what they long for their own ministries to be and what in fact can be achieved within the structure. The disillusioned clergyman is one of the tragic witnesses to this dichotomy, and there are many of them around. Goodheartedness is no substitute for disciplined theology channeled into confrontation with the world's needs.

The solution adopted by many ministers, whether we like to admit it or not, is to escape into the system, to retreat into the role which society is happy for them to play. It is a role for which too many ministers are prepared by the institutionalized training that they have been given. If he conforms, the clergyman will get his discounts from the drugstore; he will receive many fringe benefits from grateful parishioners. The fate of the clergyman who breaks away from conformity to public expectancy is materially less rewarding, however. People often resent the divine disturbance of the priest who refuses to become a mouthpiece of his parishioners' image of themselves in their Sunday clothes.

In a recent letter to alumni, the then principal of an English seminary, Bishops' College, Cheshunt, quoted from an article in the *Church Quarterly Review*. He offered some pertinent comments on the confusion of many who may be considering a vocation to the full-time ministry of the Church. The same questions would apply to many who already are ordained.

First, sociological—confusion about the role of the priest in modern society, where so much of his traditional work seems to have been taken over by others who are professionally trained, with skills and techniques of pastoral care, and with a more clearly defined job. Is there any place left for the priest, and especially for the parish priest, in modern society? And, secondly, theological—with the 're-discovery of the laity' and the increasing emphasis upon the truth that there is but one true Priest, Christ Himself, and that the priesthood of Christ is exercised by His whole priestly Body, the question is increasingly asked, "What is the need to set some men aside for ordination, particularly for a full time ministry?" It seems to me that there is little doubt that these two questions are the basic ones, and the ones which cause many men to hold back from committing themselves to an occupation which to many is sociologically ambiguous and theologically questionable.[1]

One of the challenges presented to the layman in his revolt is to help rescue his parish priest from a very similar prison of confusion and uncertainty in which he himself has been incarcerated for so long.

Among the most dangerous products of professionalism in its worst sense is the grotesque idea of a separate spirituality for clergy and laymen. This accounts for what has been a spiritual inferiority complex on the part of the laity. It is a wholesome thing to set an example of what the prayer life can be, and that is most certainly a prime task of the clergyman. It is a prime task, however, which is fast becoming a victim of the diminishing amount of time which many clergymen spend at their prayers. The laity for their part must recognize the priority of this function of their clergy. A watchful eye should always be on the demands which the parish as a whole makes upon the clergyman, diverting him from the ultimate source of the strength of his ministry.

---

[1]Quote by the Rev. Canon Philip H. Cecil from *Church Quarterly Review*, July-September, 1966.

It is an entirely different matter, however, when prayer becomes departmentalized, with one department for the clergy and another for the laity. "Father So-and-So's Mass" is not just a slipshod expression; it is a description of what both Father So-and-So and his parishioners are prepared to accept as a fact. Christian spirituality involves man's relationship with God through prayer. It requires real awareness of that neglected side of our nature which has stamped upon it the divinity of the God in whose image we are made.

Prayer is prayer, whether of the laity or clergy. Both share in the identical need for God. The prayer of the priest is no loftier than that of the humblest layman, and God's response to it is no more or less generous. Whether in public or private worship, all men are able to transcend their humanity through the incredible two-way communication receiver set built into each of us. In public and in private worship we speak with God and we listen to Him. In the sacraments of the Church we receive the life-giving strength and power of God in their different forms, each accommodating specific needs of our lives. The ordained clergyman is set apart through the vocation God has given to him, as God's human agent through which grace is channeled to men. The layman, too, in what in a very real sense was his ordination at his baptism, is set apart to exercise his particular ministry in the light of the talents given to him and the use to which those talents can be put by God. The Eucharist is Christ's offering of Himself, in which we all participate, by which all are fed.

I must admit that Church services as usually found have begun to present a very real problem to me. I really feel for the captive audience on so many occasions. Here again is an attribute of the wrong sort of clerical professionalism at which I urge the laity to strike. Often, Church services contribute to the idea that prayer is the department of the professional clergy. The very way we tend to do things in Church raises the assumption that what is going on is the clergyman's business. If we are to continue with our little professional pieces of ecclesiastical whimsy, "no trespass" signs may as well be put up in our sanctuaries with the notice pointing outward to the congregation. The signs and movements which mean not a thing to the average congregation, frequently, one suspects, mean little more to the clergyman himself.

The function of the minister in public worship is to lead his people in prayer, and if God is the object of the exercise then the clergyman should be as unobtrusive as possible. One of the reasons often advanced for the use of vestments is to obscure the personality of the priest. On occasions, however, one is led to think that the object of the vestments is to make the priest as conspicuous as Richard Burton playing the part of Becket, during which the "extras" of choir and congregation must not get in the way of the camera. (In addition, in our visual presentations we are far removed from the excellence which Mr. Burton brought to his ceremonial scenes.)

Public worship essentially involves congregational participation, otherwise the Church service might as well offer a matinee performance of a religious theater group. But congregational participation is often the very last possibility open to our long-suffering people. It is not edifying to sit through often unintelligible mumblings, the eucharistic rapid-fire of a priest who can celebrate in fifteen minutes flat, and the caterwauling of many clergymen who should accept the fact that a service well spoken is more meaningful than one badly sung. If only the laity would strike a blow at our pomposities, then perhaps Church services might inspire the layman to translate public worship into individual witness for the rest of the week.

Times of services are often something else which the layman has every right to complain about, unless he falls into the erroneous assumption that midweek services are the private fraternity meetings of the clergy. It is almost as if there was a conspiracy on the part of professionals to have either no services at all during the week or to have them at such inaccessible hours that the average lay person, even if he wanted to, could not hope to attend. Early morning metabolism and spirituality somehow have become confused.

For some strange reason, the idea has taken root, and is illustrated on nearly every church notice board one sees, that God goes off duty after seven in the morning. How on earth the housewife with a couple of children to get off to school, with breakfast to cook for the entire family, can be expected to attend a seven o'clock Eucharist on a Wednesday morning is beyond my understanding. Somehow anchored to a distant bucolic past, near-sunrise services are still the general order of the day. With the invention of electricity, a new era could dawn; services might be expressly designed to accommodate the people of God upon their return from work, but this provision generally seems to have escaped our attention. Mercifully, the practice of evening communions is growing.

So the laity have little to lose but their chains, and it is up to them to strike at the flabbiness of the Church wherever this is seen. Times of church services, relevance of church services, content of sermons, inarticulate mumblings, distracting professional pieties, and, yes, choral performances which completely exclude congregational participation in services designed for that purpose—all these are prime areas at which the lay revolt must strike.

Other targets for lay intervention could well be insistence that the clergy teach a relevant prayer life, both public and private; that regular Bible classes are provided and relate to everyday life; that parish priorities and structure be re-evaluated to provide for adequate training and a sound spiritual foundation for lay men, women, and children to exercise their ministry in the world. There isn't any time to lose if the layman is to be the spearhead of the Church's onslaught of concern for the world.

The following objectives are suggested as immediate areas of mission for the emancipated lay apostolate.

(1.) *The growth of a personal prayer life fortified by the fellowship of the Christian community in the Church's sacraments.* Unless our spiritual capacities are constantly being expanded and put to good use, our outreach will become atrophied in self-concern. The effect of an inverted prayer life is rather like that of having no prayer life at all. It leads to the sort of dissipating activism in housekeeping activities which has been our plague for so long. Within the context of stewardship, our time and talents can be reassessed and redirected by the God to whom we listen and speak. Prayer *is* mission and mission *is* ministry.

(2.) *The practical application of the sacrament of the present moment in our personal and public lives.* The sacrament of the present moment is one of those gloriously simple concepts of the prayer life which in practice leads inevitably to Christian action. It means the use of our wills, freely offering and dedicating to God all that we do and think and say at the time of commission. If this spiritual trigger mechanism is constantly applied, then the words that I speak can become the expression of what Christ would have me say in any given situation. The letters I write, the food I prepare, the work that I do, the love that I make, the song of my laughter, and the hurt of my tears—all would become living expressions of the Christ indwelling me. In time, there develops a spontaneity of Christ-reference in all situations as they arise. Whether we be clergy or laity, man, woman, or child, and however busy we may be, the sacrament of the present moment can be applied. Such application brings Christ into every aspect of life.

When I begin to see myself, my neighbor, and the world in which I live with the eyes of Christ, I long to release His love and power indwelling me, to heal the wounds of a world which does not often recognize His presence. This is an action program which springs not out of a committee but from the spirit. It can lead those of us who honestly and humbly seek to respond to Christ's imperatives into the strangest places and situations where the institutional Church is not to be found.

(3.) *The Christian community must reach outside itself.* Any parish can be revitalized if the laity apply to their real function in it the devotion applied by members of the Rotary and similar clubs to their purpose. Many secular organizations put us to shame by their efficiency, dedication, and creative activity. A dynamic spiritual life will not result in a passive response by Christians to social needs. Just a few lay people "on fire" could make any parish come alive. The source of that life would be the power of God, in whose strength mountains of injustices, intolerance, bigotry, selfishness, and fear could be moved. If every parish organization were to be re-evaluated in the light of mission, many would be found redundant. The yardstick of all our activity must be mission. The domestic concerns of the Church will remain, and need to be handled efficiently and well, but that their role is secondary should be established. We must be free and mobile, and, so far as organizations are concerned, the Church should travel light.

(4.) *Fearless witness in applying the consequences of our faith inside and outside our own lives.* This applies to business as well as to home, in factory as well as in church, in both our public and our private morality. The laymen must be equipped to deal with the hostility generated by what the world will regard as the intrusion of piety, from which it has been long preserved, into its inner life. When either layman or priest really presents a living Christ in his life, he will get hurt; not only by the ridicule and often the isolation of friends downtown, but also by fellow members of the Church.

In a country such as South Africa, many illustrations of the consequences of Christian witness can be given, and similar consequences will result elsewhere. He is a brave layman indeed who, in South Africa, will stand up and be counted for the dignity of all men regardless of race or color. (The words, "fear not little flock" [Lk. 12:32], take on meaning for Anglicans when a cabinet minister can refer to us as "the most hated Church in Africa.")

The difficulties of non-white Christians in South Africa are considerable and are rightly advertised in the world. The white Christian has problems too, which are not so apparent. It becomes very difficult for a white layman to be loyal to his Church when he is under constant attack and ridicule because of his membership of it. The easy thing for him to do is to anesthetize principles by constant compromise with expediency. To opt out and then to rationalize the option by the retention of social acceptability is a real temptation. The good, loyal, white, Christian South African is the salt of the earth, because his loyalty to Christ costs something, and to pay such a price his conviction has to be sure; it has to be based upon something infinitely deeper than humanitarianism. Many fine men and women who do not even profess the Christian faith show a much greater sensitivity and courage in the face of the evils of apartheid than do the overwhelming majority of white Christians. After all, the majority of those who elect the government which perpetrates the blasphemy of apartheid would claim to be Christian, and in order to vote a person must be white. In South Africa, many non-Christians, together with the dwindling Christian remnant, provide by their witness to justice in the face of oppression and persecution an inspiration to a world in which apathy reigns supreme.

Wherever fearless witness is the hallmark of faith in action, all the spiritual and material help which the Church can provide is required. This applies to the United States, north or south, to Britain, or to South Africa, or wherever Christian witness is a costly privilege.

In the United States and in Britain, an increasing number of courses, retreats, and programs are geared for the laity. The layman must insist that these look outward into the world. If they look inward they will merely professionalize the restriction of his existing involvement in the periphery concerns of the Church. Christianity must fight to survive in a world which is totally unaffected by the organization of potluck suppers.

And so the time for revolution is here. The movement has already begun, and the Church is wide open for redefinition of the role of the layman in a new-found vision of the lay apostolate. In his vocation to be a minister of Jesus Christ, the layman's task is to see that the fire does not go out, and to get on with the job in hand. This is not the time to be put off by the Alice-in-Blunderland maze of professional prerogatives. Christ's longing to conquer men's hearts through love in an estranged world is far too serious and urgent for that.

XI

STOCK IN TRADE—A
COLLAR IN MY BRIEFCASE

THE CHURCH is mission, and mission means nothing less than the total expression of Christ's continuing ministry to people. Clergy and laity alike make up this servant ministry. Another interesting development showing the shape of things to come is the increasing number of men offering themselves for the supplementary ministry of the Church. It may reasonably be assumed that there will always be the need for the full-time sacerdotal ministry of the Church. This need will remain for as long as God chooses to call men to such a ministry. The full-time, visible, sacerdotal ministry will remain for so long as men respond to God's call. We must not forget, of course, that our earthly, visible priesthood is the temporal expression of Christ's own priesthood committed to the hands of men. What we exercise is Christ's authority committed to His Church. Both Church and priesthood depend upon Christ Himself as the source of their existence and power. The assumption therefore that a sacerdotal ministry is of the essence of the Church's life is a theological one, a fact of history and of Christian experience.

We may also assume that the need of the laity to express their Christian faith in and through their vocation and talent will remain and indeed grow as men learn to respond to God's specific and personal calls. This assumption too is a theological one, and is based on Christ's continued action in the world. The lay vocation to Christian mission, although so long wrapped in a cocoon, is a continuing one, and is itself an extension of Christ's redemptive work. The lay apostolate has always existed and will remain as a fact of Christian life, whether or not the Church, at any given time, recognizes this. In other words, the ministry of the laity is not a new feature of the divine economy—it is a forgotten asset which has been carried on the Church's books for centuries, always tucked away in fine print. With our developing understanding of lay apostolate and its place in mission and total ministry, it could become the vehicle of Christ's most visible activity in the world.

Yet there is a third and growing outlet of vocation sometimes referred to as the supplementary ministry. No single term adequately gives to the concept a right perspective. Like "part time priesthood," the term, "supplementary ministry," is in danger of being misunderstood. If a man is a priest, then he is a priest in the whole Church. Functionally, the part-time priest will supplement the work of the full-time professional. Yet his ministry shares the same priesthood of Jesus Christ. We must be very careful, therefore, in our examination of this development in the concept of the ministry, not to ascribe any inferior quality to the priesthood of a man who earns his living, as did St. Paul, outside the professional ministry. Maybe there are second-class people who exercise it, but there is no second-class ministry which has its source in Jesus Christ.

In some places, as a consequence of the dwindling supply of men who are willing and financially able to devote themselves exclusively to the full-time ministry, the supplementary ministry has grown as the child of necessity. Many a late vocation has been lost because of financial commitments which have built up over the years. Often, in the case of a family man, such a consideration completely precludes him from changing his job on the strength of which he has structured his own and his family's life. It is not the slightest good being over-pious about such a situation and saying, "If a man really loves his God and his Church, he will sacrifice anything to serve as a priest." It is extremely dubious that the God "unto whom all hearts be open, all desires known, and from whom no secrets are hid," really calls a man into a condition of life which prac-tical circumstances make impossible. The ministry is neither a practical impossibility nor an escape hatch for financially overcommitted laymen. What the supplementary ministry cer-tainly does offer is an opportunity for otherwise frustrated vocations to be realistically accepted. In a sense, it removes many of the blocks in the way of our response to God's will for us. The range of God's call is widened, so to speak.

It would be a pity, however, if this development were to be merely tolerated as simple expediency. Properly nurtured and channeled, it could grow into a more mature awareness of the nature of the ministry itself. The fusion of the sacred and secu-lar would be manifest in the persons of those validly called to a dual vocation. It would be tragic if our experiments in this form of ministry were to become halted or even slowed down by the professional braking mechanisms which so readily are applied to the Church's ministry. Acceleration would seem more to be the order of the day.

For a long time, the priest-schoolmaster has been accepted in a dual vocation which properly has become fused in the ministry of the dissemination of truth. The priest-doctor is an-other example of a very proper fusion of Christ's concern for the whole man in the ministry of healing which is to both body and soul. The overseas mission field has benefited richly from these instances of dual vocation, and now we appear to be on the verge of a considerable extension of the formula.

If the priest-schoolmaster and the priest-doctor are accepted in a duality of vocation, why not the priest-lawyer, the priest-labor-union executive, the priest-factory worker, the priest-businessman—all exercising Christ's ministry both within their secular employment and sacerdotal calling? There is a wealth of involvement with society here which cannot be ignored. The administration of justice, a person's labor with hands or mind, or his contribution to commerce, are all activities through which God works, and through which man can grow into a fuller expression of what he was born to be. There are, of course, increasing instances of this fusion actually taking place. It is still a very tender plant in the vineyard, however, and needs to be nurtured with great care if it is not to be killed either by kindness or neglect.

What is now needed is much wider acceptance of the validity of dual vocation. We do not seek ways of finding cut-price priests, but rather the release of vocational power where it is most needed, right in the heart of downtown.

The supplementary ministry should not be confused with the worker-priest movement in the Roman Catholic Church in France, or in the few Anglican experimental situations such as the automobile factories of Oxford, England. The supplementary ministry is approaching the problem from the other direction. We see lay vocation working inward to fuse with the sacerdotal expression of it, rather than the professional priest working outward from his priesthood to incorporate secular employment. Instead of the specialist priest applying his ministry to a secular situation, the specialist layman is applying the experience of his secular vocation to the ordained ministry.

In the fusion of both movements, Christ, who is the totality of all ministry, is released incarnationally into the world. His healing power is directed to where the world's pain and separation hurt the most. The effect in both cases, however, is very similar, and a self-supporting ministry is being evolved. As was found in the institutional and hierarchical pressures brought to bear on the Roman Catholic priest-workers in France, the danger is that our professionally oriented structures might well curb the capacity for experimental ministry inherent in the freedom of financial independence.

In South Africa, several dioceses have embarked upon carefully defined programs of training and deployment of men who are called to a dual vocation. There are obvious and real dangers against which all concerned must be on guard. The supplementary ministry could become a flood gate releasing troubled waters. There is a possibility that men, academically and psychologically unsuitable for the full-time ministry, with its long period of training and evaluation, would come in by the back door of easy admission. The vocational testing necessary for men offering themselves for the supplementary ministry must be as rigorous as that applied to men entering seminaries. The training program must be thorough and long, but custom-made for the needs of men whose training can be only part time. Wherever possible, even if during vacations, trainees should spend some time in a seminary to gain community experience of worship, learning, and fellowship. Care, of course, must be taken to ensure that creeping clerical professionalism does not subordinate the ministry to the world to that of inward-looking institutional structures. The stability of a man offering himself for the supplementary ministry in his own community should be established, because there will be obvious difficulties if a man is likely to move to a different city or diocese. Once he is ordained, he is a priest of the whole Church, but, in the case of a part-time priest financially independent of the Church, a bishop cannot exert anything like the pastoral or jurisdictional authority as he can in the case of a full-time man. At the same time, there could be advantages in this comparative freedom from hierarchical control. Too often the bishops themselves have applied the brakes to change and to progress. Rather like absent landlords from everyday life, some members of the hierarchy have exercised long-range control over experimental ministry. Much development over the years has been inhibited by undue caution and conservatism at the top, which only in very recent times shows signs of changing. Obviously, there must be an ordered transition if our new enlightenment is not to dissipate itself in chaos. Order, however, should be the servant and not the master of transition.

Although there are many complications, dangers, and problems to be overcome, the supplementary ministry offers real potential growth in our awareness of what the ministry is. Essentially, it is a pioneer type of ministry. Yet it is one which, at the same time, can both reinvigorate the professional clergy by the addition of new blood, and extend, far beyond the possible reaches of the professionals, the Church's sacramental ministry into the secular world. Such a fusion of sacred and secular will bring a little nearer the great leap forward which the Church must make if she is to survive.

There is, of course, a corollary to all of this with which we must begin to grapple. This is the case of the full-time priest (or bishop, as in the case of Bishop Pike) who feels called to a full-time vocation outside what many would regard as his priesthood. It is perfectly conceivable that a priest may feel called to study medicine, or to become a full-time university professor. A priest's interests in the behavioral sciences conceivably might cause a shift in vocational emphasis and compel him to become a psychiatrist. We cannot overlook the possibility that, just as God calls a lawyer to be a priest, so He may call a priest to be a lawyer. In the past, in such a case, the impression would have been given that the only course would be to renounce the ordained ministry. At this stage, we can do little more than question this. It is, however, a reverse question that must be raised in any examination of the validity of the supplementary ministry.

Do spiritual growth and vocational awareness lead a person solely to the professional ministry? Of course we would give an emphatic negative to any such suggestion. Quite properly, it is constantly emphasized that the vocation of the Christian layman is to exercise Christ's ministry within his own calling and talents. Because of the central position of the professional clergy in the Church, there has always been the danger that the layman may be led to believe that his is an inferior vocation; that when a man "goes into the Church" inevitably he offers himself for the ordained ministry. We have seen some of the bitter harvest of the qualitative distinction between the clerical and lay vocation which only now is being broken down. On no account must the supplementary ministry become the vehicle of our return to this qualitative dichotomy of the ministry of Christ. And so, with this in mind, we must raise the possibility that the supplementary ministry might be called to handle two-way traffic—laymen fusing the secular vocation with the sacerdotal ministry in one direction, and, in the other, priests moving outward to develop a "secular" vocation in business, industry, or the professions. The essential fact is that the meeting point of both movements is still the ministry of Christ.

It could well be that the supplementary ministry of the Church may house a professional priest whose duality of vocation takes him outside the full-time priesthood into a "secular" occupation. In such a case, assuming that the man who is already ordained still feels called to exercise his priesthood, why can't he be a supplementary priest? If the same ordination service is to be used for both supplementary and full-time clergy, a question might be raised on the matter of the Church's intention when a man is ordained. In the Episcopal Church, the bishop expresses his "good hope" that the candidate has "clearly determined, by God's grace, to give yourselves wholly to this Office, whereunto it hath pleased God to call you: so that, as much as lieth in you, ye will apply yourselves wholly to this one thing, and draw all your cares and studies this way. . . ."[1] It would seem that our enlarged awareness of the nature of "this Office," in the context of Christ's whole ministry, will become increasingly significant and relevant. The point is that if the ordination service can accommodate a man retaining his secular work, why can it not equally accommodate an already ordained priest who does not find that it lies within him to exercise a full-time sacerdotal ministry? Again, little fuss is made when a priest leaves a parish to become a full-time schoolteacher or university professor. It would seem that an extension of this latitude to other Christian spheres of activity would completely remove the fear in many priests that the only alternative to remaining a full-time priest is renunciation of orders. Perhaps this applies more outside the United States, but the issue is one that must arise and be resolved.

So often it appears as though we see the ministry in terms of social "class." Certain jobs of a professional nature are considered compatible with the dignity of a priest. The switch of collars is tolerated so long as both are white. This sort of thinking is outdated and theologically unsound. It is to be hoped that more full-time professional priests will seek employment within the widest possible range of "secular" work. There is almost an immediate reaction on the part of many bishops to fear that a priest wishing to take secular employment has "lost his vocation." My own feeling is that maybe his vocation has

---

[1] *The Book of Common Prayer*, "The Ordering of Priests," p. 541.

been enlarged and that this should be encouraged. For more priests to leave the full-time ministry and work as priests in "the world" could be as healthy a sign of growth in vocation as for more men to become "weekend priests."

The growth of supplemental ministry is a much-needed shot in the arm. Provided that it is handled with care, both to preserve its freedom to develop and to preserve necessary order in the Church, it can give much needed new life to the Church of the new order. It deserves to be seriously encouraged and carefully nurtured. Through it, the Church may be more able to move with the times in which today, like all other times in history, God continues through Christ to redeem His world.

XII

MORALITY AND THE NEED TO LOVE

W E HAVE DISCUSSED at some
length the need for drastically changed priorities and structures
in the institutional church if her mission is to be effective.
Equally in need of re-examination are fundamental attitudes
which, because they seem to be so out of touch with life today,
provide considerable inhibitions to the serious attention of the
world. An area of life in which the Church's attitude is most
at variance with that of secular society is sex. If we are to communicate, reverently and effectively, Christian teaching on
human sexual relationships, the urgency of our need to update
our knowledge of the subject is obvious. Such updating may,
of course, lead to changes of accepted norms of behavior, however firmly entrenched such norms may be.

To say this does not mean that the Church should adjust her
teaching to the lowest common denominator of what is accept-
able to contemporary social standards of behavior. When we
speak of morality we are not discussing a cost-of-moral-living
index with a sliding scale of values. Christians, like everybody
else, should see moral values in the light of what God has revealed about man's personality and the human condition. Such
revelation will come through our personal experience in life as

well as through scientific knowledge. Our allegiance to truth is not relative but absolute. It is well said that if we love God, who is truth, then we can do whatever we like. What can and should change is our perception of what the truth of any situation is. As Christians, we have as strong a commitment to search out truth as we have to live by the truth which we discover and are able to accept.

Incalculable damage has been done, mainly no doubt through ignorance, by those who have clung on tenaciously to moral precepts which no longer can claim the basis of fact. Nowhere is evidence of this state of affairs more clearly to be seen than in some of the self-examination cards which use a check-list method of preparation for confession. The implications of such a simplistic "did you?" or "didn't you?" approach can be really rather frightening. The inflexible approach to behavior may well have created far more demands upon a psychiatrist's time than it has preserved for the priest.

A case in point is masturbation. Variously described as "playing with oneself" or "self-abuse," the question of masturbation is framed with euphemistic evasion to the intending penitent. On the rare occasions the subject is mentioned at all, the dire consequences of masturbation, ranging from blindness to insanity, were, and, it is feared, still sometimes are, emphasized. To many a small boy, masturbation has assumed the proportion of the unforgivable sin. Full-grown men have been known to suffer from the hangover of this error. More than one clergyman, admittedly in somewhat conservative society, when asked whether the subject of masturbation was discussed by him with girls as well as boys in sex education classes, has given as the reason why he did not do so the assumption that girls do not indulge in the practice.

One would like to think that such naïveté was strictly pre-Kinsey. It cannot be claimed that Christian teaching regarding this habit, which at some time or another is indulged in by the vast majority of people, has been very helpful in the past. Much more damage has been caused by the inculcation of unnecessary guilt than ever could have been caused by the practice of masturbation. Indeed, a fair case could be made out that many of the bad effects attributed to the habit should be laid at the door of the guilt unnecessarily produced by unenlightened teaching.

Today, we know much about the habit of masturbation, its causes and effects. We know that neither physically nor psychologically is damage likely to the masturbator. To put the fear of God into children or adults through grossly unfactual consequences might well endanger emotional health much more than the perfectly natural practice can do; certainly the teaching of a right and holy fear of God is seriously jeopardized. The fact is that many psychiatrists are prepared to emphasize the positive benefits of masturbation both psychologically and often physically, too.

In the case of masturbation, as in other areas of human behavior, much moral theology has grown around totally inadequate knowledge of both the human body and the human mind. Christian commitment to truth is absolute in human behavior as in every other department of life. The theories of theology are not sacrosanct. Like everything else, they are subject to review and, where modern knowledge indicates, to change as well. We can hardly wonder at the world's reluctance to take us seriously if we continue to churn out moral guidebooks based on "facts" that every schoolboy (and girl) knows to be medieval. They may be quaint, but they are hardly the basis for teaching a modern way of life.

Enlightened concern at the wide gulf existing between the traditional position of the Church on behavior between the sexes and that practised by society has been expressed by the

British Council of Churches. A high-powered working committee was appointed with the following terms of reference:

> To prepare a Statement of the Christian case for abstinence from sexual intercourse before marriage and faithfulness within marriage, taking full account of responsible criticisms, and to suggest means whereby the Christian position may be effectively presented to the various sections of the community.[1]

Toward the end of 1966, the committee produced a report entitled *Sex and Morality*, which, although "received" by the British Council of Churches, drew fire from many quarters because of its alleged failure to give unqualified condemnation to extramarital sexual intercourse. The intention of the document was not to condemn but to try to understand what in fact is happening increasingly. The intention was praiseworthy, because it marked a vital step in Christian dialogue with the world.

The moment we enter into dialogue on the subject of sexual relationships we find attentive participants. In the first place, we are discussing profound needs experienced by every normal human being. Again, we are involved in an area of life which is exploited at almost every step a person takes in the world. Whether it be through lingerie ads in the subway, glossy magazine covers, mini skirts, or the movies, one of the phenomena of our time is the commercialization of sex. Overtly, or subliminally, the advertising industry has found a winner, and sex sells vodka with the same *élan* as it sells cars and instant credit. Almost every mass appeal is influenced by a basic assumption that sex is interesting, respectable enough to be commercial but naughty enough to be eye-catching. Above all, so far as our deepest interests are concerned, sex is very well connected.

---

[1] *Sex and Morality*, S.C.M. Press, Ltd., London, and The Fortress Press, Philadelphia, 1966, p. 5.

The emancipation of social attitudes to sex has caught the Church on the wrong foot. In the first place, in many parts of the world, "religious" people still just do not talk about sex. Secondly, what the Church has to offer in the way of teaching about sex has been given the appearance of such rigidity that the behavioral sciences now speak to moral issues with an authority which the Church, at least ostensibly, once possessed.

For centuries, the Church has offered a package deal in morality which the world quite obviously has not bought. To the outsider, she looks to have gone off into a sulk of self-righteous indignation. The practice of the new morality is very much with us, and what to do with it we just do not seem to know. In the United States particularly, where superficial candor is a national pastime, there are many instances of dialogue between Church and society on the subject of sex. Any college chaplain would place the subject high in his programing. As we have seen in other areas of ministry, this is forced upon him by the pastoral demands of the college situation. At the University of California at Los Angeles, the pastoral questions with which I was most frequently called to deal directly involved sex in theory or in practice, and the same is true, I am sure, on the campuses of most American and English schools. But our involvement is an interaction with society in which we have more to learn, perhaps, than we have to offer.

The direct involvement of the American churches with all the social bewilderment and confusion over sex is by no means duplicated everywhere else. As far as the Anglican Church is concerned, our stuffiness is most seen in this area. Whatever may be our motives, and I am trying to look at this from the point of view of the outsider, the impression we communicate in our dealing with the sex revolution is first of all to shout against it and, if this doesn't bring it to an end, then to retire into silence. We perform the classic ostrich act, and hope that the new morality will pass us by—preserving at least the virginity of the Church's attitude, if not that of most of its members. Of course, we have an easy way out—our dislike of controversy! As often as not, in most countries, the institutional Church's attitude to sex is that sex is controversial, and that controversial matters shouldn't be discussed by the Church.

Occasional religious noises are made when something threatening to established attitudes happens, or is said. For instance, correspondents in both the English *Church Times* and *The Church of England Newspaper*, following Bishop John Robinson's evidence in the *Lady Chatterley's Lover* trial, promptly manned the barricades; the rallying cry of blasphemy was called, and the alarm was sounded. Bishop Robinson had seen something of the sacred in the illicit sex relationship between Lady Chatterley and her lover, as portrayed by D. H. Lawrence. What really provoked the storm, however, was Dr. Robinson's use of the words "holy communion" to illustrate for Christians the sacredness of the relationship in the view of the non-Christian Lawrence. In the bishop's evidence at the trial, there was a probing for expression to communicate the sort of outreach and understanding which is not often seen. When the Church in the person of a bishop moves outside her castle and becomes involved, incarnationally we might say, in an entirely secular frame of reference, the shots will tend to come from behind, not from the front.

Bishop Robinson stepped outside the security of easy and platitudinous condemnation and tried to enter into dialogue and understanding. This, of course, is a tremendously difficult and dangerous thing to do. Not because the Christian need necessarily discard the traditional content of morality, but because the outreach of understanding involves listening to what those who disagree with us have to say. When in practice this involves listening to the vast majority of the world, the tendency is to feel threatened. This is hardly a holy fear. It reflects our own uncertainties as to what in fact we do believe and have to offer, rather than a strength of conviction in our case. Because of Bishop Robinson's statements given in evidence at the trial, he was referred to by the then Archbishop of Canterbury, Dr. Fisher, as "a stumbling-block and a cause of offence to many." To the world, however, the stumbling-block has been an ethical system which has become formalized, dehumanized, and apparently unworkable.

Happily, the legal action failed to have *Lady Chatterley's Lover* banned. Vindicated was the freedom to choose to read or not to read the book, as was the freedom to assess its morality or immorality by the values we accept and apply. There was given to the Church a great opportunity to move from the area of condemnation into the highly competitive arena of influencing attitudes, of offering moral content to the capacity for value judgment which is inherent in our free will.

The way to influence moral attitudes is not spontaneously to condemn whatever we do not understand. This type of moral reflex action completely precludes interaction. We seem to be so totally vulnerable, not always in what we have to say necessarily, but in the way we usually seem to say it. We talk as though there was some inbuilt predisposition on the part of society to treat seriously what we have to say, without us having to prove our involvement or concern with those who have been taught to look for the teacher's credentials.

Monica Furlong, in a recent book, writing as a concerned Anglican laywoman, has some pertinent things to say:

> A priesthood which cares only for truth needs to have less encouragement to protect the flock . . . and much more encouragment to expose people to more difficult kinds of think-

ing, more strenuous forms of culture and more passionate forms of loving.[2]

As Bishop Robinson tried to speak with love to a bewildered world, so Miss Furlong seeks to speak with love to a confused Church. Both world and Church, if wise, will listen to what each has to say. Right now, both need all the help which articulate cross currents can offer.

Another book which articulates how the professional and institutional Church is viewed by the institutionally unattached layman is *The Comfortable Pew*, by Pierre Berton.[3] Mr. Berton was an Anglican but now attends no church. His book was commissioned by the Anglican Church in Canada, and the author was invited to make a critical examination of the Church from the "outsider's" point of view. As with Bishop Robinson, considerable pressures to silence him were brought to bear by many Church groups. The dismay of many Christians was shown when sex was taken out of its wrappings. It is to the credit of the Anglican Church in Canada that *The Comfortable Pew* was published despite the many protests. In this book, we see ourselves as others see us. Whether we like it or not, the institutional Church looks pretty sick to the outsider, concerned enough as Mr. Berton is to speak to us at all.

For too long we have carried on a monologue relationship with secular society, fooling ourselves that we were being heard. For too long the Church has been answering questions about sex and morality which nobody has been asking. If we are to preach the gospel as it applies to man's moral behavior, then it seems obvious that we must establish contact with those

---

[2]Furlong, Monica, *With Love to the Church*, Hodder & Stoughton, London, 1965, and Forward Movement, Cincinnati, 1968, page 50.
[3]Berton, Pierre, *The Comfortable Pew*, McClelland & Stewart, Toronto, and J. B. Lippincott, Co., Philadelphia, 1965.

whom we seek to influence. If we are to preach the gospel to all nations, then, as in so many other areas, we must find man where he actually is, and talk to him there. We must let people see that Christians *do* understand the problems and that we *do* have something very positive to say to the society in which we live. The report on *Sex and Morality* presented to the British Council of Churches expresses the new climate of understanding and concern sweeping the Church.

> The Church, whatever the seeming moral certainties which it has upheld in the past, is today, we hope, in a mood to assist the search for values on which conduct can be based, rather than to convict individuals of error of sin for which their exact degree of individual responsibility is known to no human assessor.[4]

The value of the Monica Furlongs and Pierre Bertons is their honest appraisal of institutionalized Christianity from two different standpoints. One is a member of the Church and the other is not. Both speak to the failure of many professionals in appearing to be anything more than fuddy-duddies who are completely out of touch with the problems facing man in his search to express himself. The search takes place in a society in which moral values are the subjects of ever-changing interpretation.

If our moral theology is as strong as we like to think it is, then we will have to hold it up to the critical examination of those whose lives we seek to shape and influence by it. If we cannot convince them even of its relevance, then we are left with a masterpiece whose beauty cannot be seen by the observer, because it is hidden under the grime of centuries. The owner and professional critic may know its worth, but if the viewer

---

[4]*Op. cit.*, p. 54.

cannot see and appreciate it, then he is not likely to buy. Furthermore, why should he?

The facts of the sex revolution of our age have been well documented. Dr. Kinsey and a whole new school of sociological and behavioral analysts have ranged far and wide, and have covered just about everything from sex and the single girl to the biological details of seminal emission. There are very few skeletons left today in the closet of human sexual behavior.

Against this world-wide explosion of man's knowledge about himself, the world offers very little perspective within which the increasing facts of life can be morally contained. Undigested facts without moral capacity to handle them do not lead to freedom. They lead to a brightly illuminated prison camp of man's continued frustration. What the Church can do is to facilitate man's escape from overwhelming bewilderment in the use of his undirected power. Every discovery of science demands a matching growth in our capacity to use it morally. Religion offers man an opportunity to remove himself from the center of his own moral attention.

Our first step forward is to be surer than we seem to be of the basis of our moral attitudes. I am very concerned to look at this problem from the point of view of those whom we seek to influence. Too readily in the past we have acted on the assumption that Christian morality is based upon an unchanging and unchangeable moral code. This conservative position has become taken for granted. Based on the theory of natural law, we are seen from the outside to take refuge in totally binding and unchanging moral precepts, which apply to all societies past, present, and future. In this theory, the moral law is promulgated by the Church in accordance with Divine will and authority. The ground rules are absolute and are not affected either by changing social needs, or by our ever-increasing knowledge of the individual, or the social make up of man.

Thus, in such a theory, there is little room for any reinterpretation of moral theology as a consequence of scientific discovery.

The report to the British Council of Churches expresses some difficulty in accepting the extreme conservative position as the basis of the Church's moral law. Several reasons are advanced:

(a) Absolute validity can be claimed only for a small number of indisputable general principles.

(b) Moral rules do conflict and so where this happens some must be discarded in any resolution of the conflict.

(c) Our re-appraisal of the natural law tradition must harmonize with the best moral sense of our times, enlightened as they are by increased knowledge and our developing understanding of Christ's own teaching.

We must present a very confused and confusing picture to the world. It is very difficult for the "outsider" to enter into serious dialogue with us. In our apparent theoretical inflexibility the inconsistency of our departures in practice from the rigidity of moral absolutism must be quite bewildering. The moral law varies from place to place, from generation to generation.

For instance, in 1920, the Lambeth Conference of bishops of the Anglican Communion declared the use of contraceptives sinful. The Lambeth Conference of 1958 declared family planning within certain clearly defined circumstances to be an obligation. Our taking for granted of slavery has changed through our understanding of the doctrine of man, to the point of contemporary Christian involvement in the civil-rights movement. Similarly, our attitude to sex deviation has undergone a metamorphosis, as has our understanding of the problem of alcoholism. Both sex deviation and alcoholism are now seen and treated as diseases rather than necessarily as sins. In all these social changes, Church leadership, let it be noted, has often provided enlightened guidance, especially in legal reform.

Sex and sin are no longer equated; the single state is no longer regarded as being in itself "higher" than the married state. Each is seen as a vocation. For the individual there can be no vocation higher than that to which he is called by God. To most branches of the Christian Church, unchastity in the sense of incontinence is no longer the equivalent of one-time membership of the Communist Party when applying for a visa to the United States. When applying for U.S. citizenship, the extraordinary question is still asked, however, "Have you ever committed adultery?"

Our dialogue with society obviously will have some new ground rules when we face up to the challenge which such debate provides. The world's doubts in our ability to provide solutions for society's dilemmas will deepen whenever we retreat into the theoretical and conservative position which the Church in practice manifestly has abandoned. Christians simply do not practise what the Church preaches, which, so far as the sexual health of our constituents is concerned, sometimes perhaps is a blessing. As Mr. Berton points out in *The Comfortable Pew*:

> The Anglican Church's attitude in birth control is especially revealing, because it involves a complete 180-degree turn in its philosophy: from absolute opposition, it moved in less than half a century to a position from which it is passing resolutions demanding a change in the law which was, in the beginning, Church-inspired.[5]

Reappraisal of what has been taken for granted to be an in-

---

[5]*Op cit.*, p. 46.

violable framework of moral rules established by Divine fiat is not limited to Anglican theory or practice. The Roman Catholic Church in re-examining her long-established refusal to admit contraception as a valid Christian practice, would appear to be on the verge of some departure from traditional moral theology. Many powerful voices have been heard in recent years demanding radical modification of Rome's extreme position of theological conservatism applied to behavior. Whether or not "the pill" offers an answer to the continued objections of some moral theologians to the practice of contraception, remains to be seen. It would be tragic indeed if Rome's theological hang-up with family planning through the application of modern medical research were to jeopardize the increasing convergence of the major Christian Churches. That this might happen is far from impossible. Where sex and morality are concerned, the individual is in a unique position to evaluate the Church's understanding of the most intimate part of his life. What can be said with certainty is that the majority of Christians using modern methods of contraception within and outside of marriage will continue to increase as such methods become increasingly available and accepted.

So what are we left with? Are we to swing the pendulum of our reaction to over-rigidity? or to the opposite extreme of complete licence? Is our contribution to the bewilderment of society in handling moral choices to be based purely on acceptance of an individual's appraisal of each situation demanding moral action as it occurs? When applied to sexual relationships this would be an uncertain yardstick indeed. The forces with which we grapple are too powerful, too fundamental to our nature, too subjective to permit such private value judgment of the best interests of ourselves, of other people and of society as a whole. To love God and do what we like is indeed a profound affirmation of our freedom, but on this side of sanctity at least we need guidelines. There must be moral principles accepted by which we educate and refine our motives, and by which we evaluate our actions.

To provide these principles, and so to teach and communicate them that they are accepted freely in what we recognize to be man's need to fulfill himself, is the Church's task. To do this we must be clear about what we teach and why we teach it. From our position of sharing and participating in the human situation, we must be in a position to evaluate the capacity of our hearers to hear and to understand. The report on *Sex and Morality* puts forward a position which the majority of its working party was able to support. It seems to open a door through which we can move out of our apparent confusion. The alternative is described as a

> . . . modified conservative position. This would give considerably more weight to motives in evaluating moral action, though without adopting the radical thesis that motive is the only significant criterion or that love is the only significant motive. It would seek to define the position of moral rules by saying that even if moral rules are not theoretically perfect, or exactly indicative of God's will at the deepest level, yet in many cases they provide the best guidance we have, so that for practical purposes it is rational to treat them as absolute. This policy involves no dishonesty or lack of realism; it simply endorses the verdict of Aristotle that morality can never be an exact science. . . .
>
> Developing this line of thought, it is possible to make motive and character the primary subject of moral judgment, while also giving great weight to the value of a sound moral code as an indispensable framework within which good motives and dispositions will be encouraged. However, all actual codes contain elements of greater or lesser importance; and we would suggest that some moral rules are of such weight that no code could justifiably omit them. Consequently,
>
> (a) It may be held that certain rules are for all practical purposes universally valid, so that it is never morally

justifiable to break them; and it may be held that the
rules of abstinence before marriage and fidelity within
it are of this character; or

(b) It may be held that even if such rules do not completely coincide with the rights and wrongs of each case
taken in isolation, yet they do prescribe what is normally
good for our society. In this case we may have a duty to
uphold the rule even at some sacrifice of personal liberty.[6]

Such a formula met with strong criticism when the report
was presented, because of its apparent latitude. What is "normally good for our society" establishes the social consequences
of an individual's actions. "Some sacrifice of personal liberty"
speaks to the individual's need to maintain personal freedom,
so that moral choice must not preclude an act which would
totally eliminate personal freedom. To do this would not be
good for society or for the individual. Blanket condemnation
of all sexual relationships outside of marriage I no longer find
possible. Each case involves highly complicated psychological
and motivating factors. However rarely the general rule of
chastity outside of marriage might be held to be inapplicable in
special cases, such cases will exist.

Pastorally, not only must we be prepared to accept such a
possibility, we should be trained to work within it. A marriage
licence is not a carte blanche for unbridled sex. Sex can be as
much an expression of sinful lust within a marriage as it often
is outside it. However imperfect the complete expression of
love outside of marriage may be, and it is necessarily imperfect, yet it can be a beautiful and meaningful growth experience. It can be gentle, self-giving, and alive. Such a relationship of love can be valid even outside of marriage. I believe
that grace operates within it, and that expressions of love within

---

[6]*Op. cit.*, p. 27.

it partake in the nature of a sacrament. If such an opinion appears to be heretical, perhaps the view of God which makes it seem so is itself so defective as to make charity in its highest sense impossible as a criterion of Christian judgment.

We can expect some intense debate as to what moral rules are universally valid. Cardinal Newman's dictum that controversy clarifies issues, may well give us the opportunity for clarification of this one. In this book I am more concerned with our basic attitudes and priorities than with the application of them to each individual case with which, when evolved, they must deal. Specifics, however, will have to be faced and the nature of these specifics will become clearer as we involve ourselves with the questions to which secular society provides singularly few answers.

In looking at the Church's attitudes with the "outsider" very much in mind, there are some general areas in which it seems our concern for relevance and understanding can profit from our listening and learning role. One of these concerns is the needs of man, individually and in community.

XIII

WHOLLY COMMUNION

THE BEHAVIORAL SCIENTIST can tell us much about what is happening in many different areas of life. Often he can project future happenings on the basis of scientifically applied principles. The events themselves, however, are statistics to the scientist. He does not claim to shape the future of man. If the Christian Church's claim to be a life shaping influence is to be seen as a valid one, a marriage must be effected between what often are considered to be rivals. The behavioral scientist and the Church must combine their concern for the human situation as it is now and as it could become.

Christ's life and actions witness constantly to something of which the Christian is in danger of losing sight. Man is not an island; the common humanity of man and the common Fatherhood of God make the life of man a community relationship. This is a fundmental fact in our dealing with individuals. We share humanity; it is our common denominator, and we cannot contract out of it. In our inter-relationships we are mutually interdependent and responsible. Social integration means to live in harmony with our fellow men. In political society this harmony is hedged about by laws with teeth in them. There are enforced codes of behavior which see individual freedom as essentially a part of social interdependence. The Christian community, however, although of course living in the world, sees human inter-relationship in theological and moral terms. We are members one of another; my sins and virtues affect you; we share a common Father, "our Father." As in so many other areas, the Church must look to the secular world for insights into the vital area of interpersonal relationship.

In a very real sense, Jesus was the perfect psychologist. He saw deep down into the reality of people, individually and in society. He constantly revealed understanding of what were the ruling intentions of people in their actions. He knew what is in man. The Church, by default, seems to have delegated the perfect understanding of Christ to the naturally imperfect understanding of the behavioral scientist. The "secular" psychiatrist very frequently shows a much greater insight into, and compassion for, the condition of people whom Christ handled so graciously, than do His servants who are ordained to exercise His ministry to the sick in mind and soul. The psychologist, for example, sees mental illness essentially as a disturbance of a person's relationship with himself or with other people, resulting in an incapacity to communicate and to be fulfilled. The mentally disturbed have become separated from their society and to a greater or lesser degree are imprisoned in their own private world. The future is hooked into a past from which there seems to be no escape. The Church would say that man is weighed down by the accumulation of guilt resulting from sin. He is in a state of self-centeredness from which he cannot escape by his unaided effort. His freedom lies in Christ's victory over sin and therefore death.

We see Christ as the great healer of the sick in body and in mind, as well as the spirit. He draws very little distinction between the state of sin and the state of physical and mental illness; each results in separation. Christ was concerned for the whole man.

The highest concern of the psychologist is very similar in effect to the concern of Christ. The common initial aim is shared by both, to restore the whole man to a state of integration with himself and with his fellow human beings who make up society. When such integration has been accomplished, the power to communicate is realized. Minister and psychologist each look for a balance of the human personality in an integrated wholeness. We recognize that in our interpersonal relationships we can satisfy our nature by enabling ourselves to function wholly and not in isolation and fragmentation. Our pastoral link with the behavioral sciences in our attempt to influence moral behavior is our shared concern for the well-integrated and fulfilled person.

In dealing with man in his community relationship, we have much to learn from the psychologist and especially the group therapist. In placing man in his relationship with God, the scientist has a great deal to learn from the Church in our showing forth of Jesus Christ who was the prototype of the complete human being. Because He was totally aware of Himself and His identity, Jesus was able to live in complete harmony with reality; hence His profound insight into human personality. The Son of Man knew Himself. His self knowledge passed the threefold test by which all knowledge must be confirmed: revelation, reason, and experience.

Applying all this to the Christian community, we see that our failure lies in our apparent inability to establish effective points of contact through meeting the profoundest needs of men. Illumination and reason are not enough by themselves to effect the charismatic encounter of real relationship. There must be also the real life experience of the healing power of love. We sometimes complain that man's isolation from the

Church and his rejection of our moral codes is voluntary. Our share of the responsibility for his isolation can be seen in a simple example. Let us take the case of a woman taken in adultery (Jn. 8:3-11).

Christ's action in one of the most compelling stories of the New Testament was on a completely different level from that usually manifested by our structured Church congregations when one of its own members, or an outsider, is involved in a similar situation in its twentieth century setting. When Christ told the woman to go away and sin no more, He did not issue a command; He communicated to her His power through His acceptance of her as a person. His concern for her as a woman, as a human being, penetrated her personality. There was a complete absence of rejection in Christ's treatment of her, and she recognized His authority as that of a whole person. The words, "Neither do I condemn thee: go thy way" (Jn. 8:11), are some of the most beautiful words in the Bible. If only the world could hear Christians say them today and show what the words mean in practice, then it would be difficult for any-one to confuse our priorities of concern. The needs of people would demand our attention.

What Jesus said and did are what most of us long to hear and see, when we are as aware of our sin as the woman taken in adultery must have been. Into all the shame and ignominy, into the very gutter of humiliation into which she had plunged, Christ reached out to her. His whole being took her and raised her to the height of acceptance as a human being. The healing power of His love's acceptance communicated to her, in a moment of time, the difference between her previous isolation and fragmentation and her new and present restoration and wholeness.

Once this difference has been seen and experienced, then and only then are we able to accept guide lines for further growth and fulfillment. The Church, of course, must seek to evolve her guide lines, but first she must achieve the relationships within her community in which the guide lines can be recognized as valid.

The trouble is that the professional Church hardly seems to know how to handle a case such as the adulterous woman. The professional psychologist tends to know much better. The Christian Church, which still numbers among its members those who dismiss psychology as something newfangled, providing competition beyond the pale, has in fact more to learn from the compassionate attitudes of medical practitioners than perhaps in any other area of the so-called secular world. Good psychology is good theology. The best theology and the most enlightened psychology both increasingly recognize that God constantly is revealing Himself through science dedicated to the understanding of human behavior. Human behavior is the hub around which man in his community revolves. The work of Dr. Frank Lake in promoting courses of clinical theology, which some 3,000 clergymen throughout the world have attended, indicates a significant breakthrough in relating pastoral ministry and contemporary psychiatry. The publication of Dr. Lake's book, *Clinical Theology*,[1] makes available a pioneering work by an eminently qualified Christian doctor who shows what the role of both clerical and lay apostolate in the field of psychiatry can become.

Contemporary developments in group therapy should be very exciting to the concerned priest and layman in the Church. Just think of a group of people possessing entirely different problems, totally different personalities, and diverse backgrounds which have created both problems and personalities. Think for a moment of such a "community," in which many

---

[1]Lake, Frank, *Clinical Theology*, Darton Longman and Todd, London, 1966.

of the blocks to interaction and communication have been removed by the assurance of being accepted and the security which such acceptance creates in one another's fellowship and company. Think of the growth toward a profound and fulfilling sense of belonging in such a group. Imagine the importance to each individual of the other members, each of whom has contributed to a greater sense of self-awareness in the others than would have been possible in isolation. Is not this an example of mutual responsibility and interdependence in terms of our human relationships? It is perfectly easy to contemplate the introduction of the woman taken in the act of adultery to a group such as this. Could the same be said for the average component of the parish community—the Mothers' Union or the Women's Auxiliary?

Surely there is much for us to learn here? At the heart of every parish there should be an inner group of concerned people who have so grown through the strength of their relationship with one another in community that the drawing power of their individual love will be seen and felt by society at large. What a social and spiritual revolution there would be if priest or layman could incorporate into an existing and accepting community those who are lifted from the spiritual gutters of this world. Whether dressed in rags or mink, those who are wretched in spirit could be assured of the depth of acceptance necessary to penetrate the agony of their isolation. The outcasts of the world are not always easily recognizable as such. They cry inside the face which is all that society is allowed to see. Nobody hears because nobody listens to the sounds beneath the surface. To see and to hear with the eyes and ears of Christ, and then to act in the power of His love, is what Christian discipleship really means. To be Christ like, we must learn to accept the unacceptable, to love the unloved and often unlovable, and to touch the untouchable. There is many a blind

Bartimaeus of this world who cries from the depth of his being, "Jesus, thou Son of David, have mercy on me" (Mk. 10:47). To hear and to respond is the Church's vocation. The point of response is where Christian priorities intersect the world's need; where the people of God cry out in pain.

Is not this task so much more relevant than the preservation of the stultified institutionalism which drains away our capacity to reach out as the accepting community? If a parish congregation is to get to know each other, maybe the parish priest must be the first to expose his real self, so that he can be loved for who he really is. The process of bearing each other's burdens is the process of real deep-down integration, because the heaviest burdens we all carry are the ones we are least likely to share. The "secular" therapy group is geared precisely to this level. The parish community should be.

The story of the woman taken in adultery shows what could become the incarnational role of the Christian community in meeting individual need at the point of social rejection. Christ meets us where we are whenever we reach out to Him. Applied discipleship necessarily creates an accepting fellowship. There is, however, another more apostolic role for the Christian community: the need to witness outside ourselves. We cannot live only to ourselves. Mere enlargement of an isolated fellowship does not meet the apostolic imperative for social involvement.

To take a practical example. What is the meaning of Christian community in any one of our cities where there is a disturbed racial situation? In applying the Christian concept of a community of love, do we in fact project this reconciling force where society is fragmented? In countries such as South Africa, Britain, and the United States, there are all too many opportunities to show the leavening power of the Christian community. If we do not show this to the world, where is

Christ's reconciling and healing power to be seen? How many churches, for instance, have asked themselves the question, "What have we done sociologically to help people visualize what the Christian community really is like?"

A Time For Burning, a fine film sponsored by the Lutheran Church in the United States, shows up the appalling weakness of Christian witness. By not translating the theory of Christian community into practice, the Church has become imprisoned in a house of glass, from which we can throw stones at society's failure only at the risk of damaging ourselves.

In the film, the basic problem is dramatically presented. A young pastor, recently arrived in Omaha, Nebraska, decides what a good thing it would be if his church were to recruit ten families from its members to visit ten families of a near-by Negro church. Such a simple idea throws his congregation into a near panic. Cleverly using the technique of *cinema verité,* the camera follows the resulting discussions among the various groups in the church, the women's group, the men's group, the trustees, and the incredible confusion is shown up. One group fears integration; another fears that there will be interracial dating among the young people. The classic prejudices about race are starkly projected; the incredible fears stirred up by an applied concept of community are poignantly portrayed.

Christian community is a challenge to be sure, and the Church cannot be blasé in assuming that the challenge will be accepted by her members. Before we can speak to the fragmentation of society in the breakdown of social community, the horrible pain of the churches' own fragmented community must be felt and suffered. It would be all too easy merely to anesthetize the pain. The cause and not the symptom must be removed, however.

In the movie, the youth bible group from the Lutheran

Church eventually invites a Negro group to meet with them on Sunday mornings. That finishes the whole business. Everyone says, "Now we see there is going to be integration." Trouble seems to be inevitable. The local mayor comes to the Church and appeals to the men to help in any way possible to produce better race relations in the city. The young pastor resigns, sorry that he ever raised the question, not having meant to divide the life of the church which now is split wide open. The impact on the viewer is jolting. He sees how pathetic the Church can be in the absence of that spiritual power which alone can overcome human doubts and enable the Church to risk something in the self-transcendence of her inverted fears.

As in the movie, time and time again the Church has failed in real life. Often it seems as though nobody comes out of such confrontations very well. Situations will continue to arise, however, and unless the Church faces up to them, she will not get very far. Corporately, and as individuals, Christians must go through the intense suffering and moral agonizing over problems which are very personal and real. Sometimes what seems to be our failure in dealing with them is the foundation of ultimate success. If we do not always work through the agony, at least we learn to face up to the suffering. Our awareness of the pain is the essential first step toward our overcoming of it. Perhaps the agonizing failure of the Church in one situation may help another church progress elsewhere. Perhaps the individual's pain, bravely borne, has on others a chain reaction which would amaze the original sufferer.

This is particularly the case in South Africa, where sometimes it seems that we are overwhelmed by the failure of the Church to show a Christian community of all races at work happily and peacefully together. Maybe our failure in South Africa can serve God's purpose in another place. In the economy of God, a voice raised in one part of the Church may only be heard in another. Never must we restrict our witness to situations in which success would seem to be assured.

Of course the world's societies are fragmented, and increasingly so. Of course the long hot summers of riots and pain will give way to the long cold winters of frustration and despair. It is small wonder that such things happen when the community of love is itself so captivated by its own fears. In our Christian dialogue with society it is a reasonable assumption that we can provide an example in practice of what we claim to offer. If we can do this, at both the individual and the social levels, the world in all its crying need may well offer to the Church the initiative for a new beginning.